WRITING THE REVOLUTION

WRITING THE REVOLUTION

WIKIPEDIA AND THE SURVIVAL OF FACTS IN THE DIGITAL AGE

HEATHER FORD

FOREWORD BY ETHAN ZUCKERMAN

THE MIT PRESS CAMBRIDGE, MASSACHUSETTS LONDON, ENGLAND

The MIT Press would like to thank the anonymous peer reviewers who provided comments on drafts of this book. The generous work of academic experts is essential for establishing the authority and quality of our publications. We acknowledge with gratitude the contributions of these otherwise uncredited readers.

This book was set in Stone Serif and Avenir by Westchester Publishing Services. Printed and bound in the United States of America.

Library of Congress Cataloging-in-Publication Data

Names: Ford, Heather, author.
Title: Writing the revolution : Wikipedia and the survival of facts in the digital age / Heather Ford ; foreword by Ethan Zuckerman.
Description: Cambridge, Massachusetts : The MIT Press, [2022] | Includes bibliographical references and index.
Identifiers: LCCN 2021058945 | ISBN 9780262046299 (paperback)
Subjects: LCSH: Wikipedia. | Egypt—History—Protests, 2011–2013—Miscellanea. | Wikipedia—Authorship. | Truthfulness and falsehood. | Semantic Web. | Google (Firm)—Influence. | Electronic encyclopedias—Cross-cultural studies. | Knowledge, Sociology of—Case studies.
Classification: LCC AE100 .F67 2022 | DDC 030—dc23/eng/20220207
LC record available at https://lccn.loc.gov/2021058945

10 9 8 7 6 5 4 3 2 1

For Luigi and Salvatore, *per sempre*

CONTENTS

FOREWORD

In March 2018, YouTube's CEO Susan Wojcicki announced that the video-sharing behemoth would begin adding excerpts from Wikipedia articles to certain videos in order to provide context. Explaining that YouTube is "not a news organization," Wojcicki told an audience at Austin's South by Southwest Conference that the website would add these "information cues" to videos about controversial topics like chemtrails, the moon landing, and other subjects popular with conspiracy theorists.[1] Rather than make challenging moderation decisions about removing this problematic content from the platform, the Wikipedia articles would ground a viewer in factual, encyclopedic reality.

In other words, YouTube decided to outsource the problem of determining what's true to Wikipedia, the web's most fascinating—and misunderstood—project.

From YouTube's point of view, this is an inspired move. Moderation is expensive, time-consuming, controversial, and only becoming more difficult to do. Determining what's true in a world that seems divided into not just rival ideological camps but rival epistemologies is a losing proposition for a business that just wants to market advertising to its two billion monthly users. Why pick a fight over the truth in Donald Trump's America, where only two years later the president would deny the existence of a global pandemic and his supporters would declare that the election that removed him from power was fraudulent?

Being held up as a noncontroversial source of truth represented a remarkable turn for Wikipedia. Ten years earlier, pundits debated whether an encyclopedia written by pseudonymous nonexperts should ever be taken seriously. Schoolteachers warned students against citing Wikipedia directly. Now one of the world's most powerful companies was admitting that, in a contentious world, Wikipedia is likely the closest we will ever get to consensus reality.

But how does Wikipedia determine what consensus reality is? And is the method of achieving consensus mysterious and technical, or is it rooted in traditional questions of influence and power?

Using one of the most remarkable factual events of the new millennium—the Egyptian revolution of 2011—as its central narrative, this remarkable book unpacks the complex and nuanced question of how Wikipedians decide what constitutes a fact. Through interviews with Wikipedians and a careful reading of the talk pages and editing records, Heather Ford offers a surprising narrative in which Wikipedia is not just a passive observer but an active player in determining our understanding of the Arab Spring.

Ford's exposition centers on the story of a single Wikipedian, whose contribution to overthrowing Mubarak was as simple and as profound as framing the events that began on January 25, 2011, as a revolution rather than a demonstration, a riot, or an uprising. Ford's careful reading of Wikipedia records shows that The Egyptian Liberal, the creator of the "2011 Egyptian Protests" Wikipedia entry, was active in framing the events in Tahrir Square as a popular uprising, a movement that was underway, an event that could lead to a revolution. Through careful crafting of an article and its metadata—and the shepherding of citations, the ammunition for policy battles on Wikipedia—The Egyptian Liberal frames the events unfolding in Tahrir Square as a continuation of the events a few weeks earlier in Tunisia, an uprising spreading through the region. Ford shows that this framing precedes the global media's understanding of what unfolds in Tahrir Square and helps certify the Egyptian revolution as fact.

Ford describes the process of The Egyptian Liberal and the thousands of other Wikipedians who contribute to the article in the tumultuous weeks after January 25 as the stabilization of facts. It is this complex, technical, and political work that shapes knowledge both on Wikipedia and in the broader world, as the facts set down in Wikipedia become Siri's and Alexa's answers to questions asked of our voice-activated devices, or the information delivered at the top of Google search results. Given Wikipedia's power for stabilizing facts and propagating them throughout the world, it is critical that we understand the processes through which events become fact.

Wikipedians—including Wikipedia's cofounder Jimmy Wales—can express a belief in the community's process, which seems as much rooted in faith as in fact. Somehow the collective action of many people contributing to a single work, unified around the community's core values of a neutral point of view, verifiability, and no original research, allows the convergence of a stable reality in an unstable and disputed world. Ford shatters this faith-based version of Wikipedia with the story of the Egyptian revolution article, written by a partisan to ensure a particular political framing of events was the version of the world that stabilized as fact.

Shattering the magic of the Wikipedia process has other implications. Faced with criticism of Wikipedia's flaws, including an overrepresentation of men over women in its biography pages and a bias toward North American and Europe over Africa and Asia, defenders of the project offer the mirror theory, the idea that Wikipedia mirrors the inequities of knowledge production of the world as a whole. But that idea is untenable once you follow Ford's exegesis. Knowledge on Wikipedia is not a reflection and distillation of knowledge available in the world, assembled by neutral actors. It's a painstaking and technical process in which Wikipedians use their understanding of the community's tools and procedures to advocate for the importance of some events over others, for preferred framings to become factual understandings that propagate throughout the world.

Ford's examination of a single Wikipedia article, then, becomes a bold new epistemology of our digital age. Long before Wojcicki decided to solve YouTube's moderation problems by relying on Wikipedia, Google had embraced Wikidata (the structured repository of facts gleaned from Wikipedia articles) as the backbone of its search results, the Google Knowledge Graph. As our world has transformed from one in which facts are written in books to one in which facts are available instantly, online, the path of a fact from the observed world into Wikipedia and then out into the world becomes the key process in understanding how our world is shaped.

Reading Ford's explanation of a fact's "allies" and "companions" and how the technosocial processes of advocating for a particular set of facts shape our collective reality, I was struck by the sheer audacity of her intellectual project. This book describes epistemology as practiced in the world today, no more or less. Rather than debating a philosophical tradition that goes back further than Aristotle, Ford simply presents the world of facts as they are today: contingent, political, and deeply dependent on a peculiar volunteer project that sits not just at the center of the web but at the center of the world and how we know it.

Wikimedia reacted to Wojcicki's elevation of Wikipedia as the arbiter of truth with bemusement and frustration, quickly making it clear that there was no formal relationship between YouTube and the volunteer project, though anyone was free to use Wikipedia for whatever purposes they saw fit. At some point, YouTube got the message and began using "context snippets" from *Encyclopedia Britannica*, presumably paying a license fee for the content.

Wikipedia is unlikely to slip away from Ford's analysis as easily. Wikipedia is remarkable, laudable, praiseworthy, and endlessly amazing. But it is not magical, and it cannot stand beyond careful scholarly scrutiny. Ford starts the important process of coming to grips with what Wikipedia is and what it is not. Her understanding of Wikipedia as a complex, beautiful, but knowable system of processes and power relationships deserves to become a stable fact.

Ethan Zuckerman
Amherst, MA
November 3, 2021

PREFACE

In mid-July 2008, I arrived in a hot and sticky Alexandria. I had traveled to Egypt from my home base in Johannesburg to attend Wikimania. As the name suggests, Wikimania is an event for those who share an all-consuming passion for the wiki. But not just any wiki . . . the most important wiki of all: Wikipedia. The annual conference for Wikipedians (Wikipedia's volunteer editors), Wikimania is an opportunity to celebrate the project, discuss important issues, and geek out on wiki lore.

I attended Wikimania as one of 650 other attendees from forty-five countries in 2008. The majority, like Wikipedians themselves, were men. But there was a smattering of women, some in key positions in the free and open source software and open content movement. I was in one of those positions at the time, although I didn't recognize that fact until much later.

That year I joined Wikimania as the executive director of iCommons and as an advisory board member of the Wikimedia Foundation, the non-profit organization that hosts Wikipedia and other open knowledge projects. iCommons and Wikipedia were indelibly linked via Creative Commons, an organization I had volunteered for when I was a resident fellow at Stanford University's (now discontinued) Digital Vision Fellowship Programme in 2003. After Stanford, I had gone back home to South Africa to cofound Creative Commons South Africa with the Intellectual Property lawyer Andrew Rens. After establishing projects to build awareness and knowledge about the value of free and open source software and open content for the African continent, I joined iCommons, first as a board member and then as the executive director.

iCommons was founded by the board members of Creative Commons, including Lawrence Lessig, Jonathan Zittrain, Joi Ito, and Wikipedia's cofounder and so-called constitutional monarch Jimmy Wales. Creative Commons had developed a set of copyright licenses for content like music, images, and books that marked them as free to copy, share, and build on. Wikipedia became Creative Commons' most significant licensor when it adopted the Creative Commons Attribution Share-Alike license in 2005.[1] Under these license terms, anyone can make a copy of Wikipedia and publish it (even for commercial purposes) as long as they attribute Wikipedia and share their copies under the same terms.

iCommons was established to lead the international movement around free culture. The iCommons Summits, held in Rio de Janeiro, Dubrovnik, and Sapporo, were heady celebrations of the creativity and innovation that could flourish from the commons. Wikimania, then, was always a highlight. I was a senior salesperson selling openness to the world. At Wikimania, I could relax. There was no one to convert. The attendees generally beat my zealousness by scores.

Winning the bid to host Wikimania attracts high prestige in the wiki universe, and Wikimania can provide a significant boost to Wikipedia editing in the host country. Wikimania was held in the Bibliotheca Alexandrina that year. Completed in 2002, the Bibliotheca Alexandrina is an attempt to revive the Great Library of Alexandria, one of the most significant libraries of the ancient world. But the conference had been mired in controversy. There were calls to boycott the event because of Egypt's censorship and imprisonment of bloggers.[2] Wikipedia cofounder Jimmy Wales promised to speak about freedom of speech and human rights in response. Perhaps Wikimania could influence the Egyptian government to improve their free speech record.

On the first day of Wikimania, a government spokesperson opened the conference. Wales, in keeping with his promise, spoke about freedom of speech and highlighted the case of Abdel Kareem Nabil, a former student at Al Azhar University. Nabil had been sentenced in 2007 to three years in prison on charges of insulting Islam and the Prophet Muhammad and inciting sectarian strife, and another year for insulting President Hosni Mubarak.

In his speech, Wales implied that the government's actions could be hampering people in the country from editing Wikipedia. Even though some governments tried to impede free speech, he said, this was pointless in the age of the internet, where people could share ideas on platforms like Wikipedia. "Kareem Amer has become a cause around the world," he said and then showed Nabil's English Wikipedia page. "Not the best strategy for keeping his ideas out of the public eye."

The Middle East was a key focus area for Wikipedia at the time. Although it was starting from a low base, Arabic Wikipedia was growing at a faster rate than English Wikipedia. There was support for Arabic Wikimedia from the Wikimedia Foundation and lots of promise for the region.

WNYC Radio's Brian Lehrer interviewed Jimmy Wales, Mohamed "Mido" Ibrahim (the lead organizer of Wikimania 2008), and Noam Cohen (the *New York Times* journalist who often covers Wikipedia and Wikimania) shortly after Wikimania 2008.[3] Mido was asked why it was important that Egypt host Wikimania that year. "The Arabic community needed it," he replied, "and we tried our best to win this conference here in Alexandria. . . . We need to spread the level of awareness of freedom of knowledge and freedom of expression."

"But Egypt is a pretty authoritarian government . . . and freedom of expression, we know, is not always tolerated so . . . why did they even allow you to do it?" asked Brian Lehrer.

Jimmy Wales replied that Egypt had "some problems" around freedom of speech, notably with bloggers being arrested. "Wikipedia, on the other hand, is viewed as neutral—we try to be neutral, we try to [share] knowledge. My own feeling is that in our own way we're much more subversive than a blogger complaining about the president because I think that this fundamental, deeper idea . . . that Mido was just speaking about, that people have a right to share knowledge, have a right to participate in the building of culture is very powerful and really has the potential to change ideas at a more fundamental level than just a question of whether or not you're allowed to criticize the president."

Two and a half years later, Egypt was on fire. I had watched, captivated, as Egyptians took to the streets in January to demand the end of authoritarian rule. Members of the free and open source software and open content movement from Egypt were involved in the protests. The blogger and democratic activist Alaa Abd El Fattah and his wife, Manal, had gone back to Egypt after living and working in South Africa to join the revolution. We had met at a free and open source software and open content workshop in Tajikistan and stayed in touch. They were thrilled about being part of what looked to be a new era in Egyptian history.

Less than two weeks later, Egypt's longtime president and autocrat Hosni Mubarak resigned after fleeing the country. The people of Egypt had achieved the unthinkable. Some were calling this "the Facebook Revolution,"[4] others a "Twitter revolution." These labels certainly overstate the role of platforms in the revolution and downplay the role of ordinary Egyptians' organizing and activism. But there was no doubt that the internet had changed Egypt. The country's state-controlled media had effectively suppressed dissident activities until that point. But the internet's relative openness enabled young Egyptians to catalyze the movement that finally toppled Mubarak.

Facebook and Twitter have been the focal points of public analysis about the role of the internet in Egypt's revolution. But at the end of January 2011, as protests were still reverberating across Egypt and Mubarak had not yet resigned, the Israeli Wikipedian Dror Kamir wrote a startling message to a mailing list about Wikipedia's role in the Egyptian protests.[5] Kamir pointed out that the first draft of the article about the revolution on English Wikipedia was published just hours after the first protests began. An Egyptian Wikipedian with the username The Egyptian Liberal had published the article not on Arabic or the Egyptian Arabic Wikipedia, his mother tongue, but on *English* Wikipedia. The article, Kamir realized, had quite obviously been prepared before the first protests and in order to influence public opinion. "It almost seems as if the article preceded the actual events,"[6] he wrote.

To Kamir, this demonstrated that Wikipedia "was losing its encyclopedic characteristics."[7] Wikipedians pride themselves on neutrality. NPOV, or neutral point of view, is a core content policy, and editors are called to merely summarize reliable sources rather than offering their own, original analysis. Policy determines that Wikipedians should *follow* public opinion rather than *lead* it. "Wikipedia is not a chrystal ball," according to the

Wikipedia policy "What Wikipedia is not."[8] In a blog post[9] a few months later, Kamir wrote that this was a case in which Wikipedia actively shaped public opinion. Wikipedia had clearly played a significant role in events, but "who is going to remember that Wikipedia played a role in this Egyptian revolution?" he wrote.

When I read Kamir's notes, I was completing my master's at the University of California, Berkeley's iSchool. I had left iCommons two years before this, increasingly skeptical about the value of openness as it had been determined by its US founders. I wanted iCommons to be a thriving organization, based in the Global South and pioneering new approaches to the commons from the perspective of the subaltern. Not everyone agreed. I was distraught. I had given everything to the movement, and it had ended without warning. I went back to school in 2009 because I didn't know what else to do. At Berkeley, I was determined to forge a path away from the free culture movement. But it kept beckoning me from unexpected locales. Perhaps I wanted to discover the argument that would break it, as it had broken me.

In late 2011, I accepted a position as ethnographer for the Kenyan nonprofit technology company Ushahidi. I was tasked with understanding what heuristics volunteers used to verify rapidly changing information from online sources. Wikipedians routinely cover breaking news events—from protests to natural disasters to pandemics—and so the site seemed to be an excellent location to study these practices. The 2011 Egyptian revolution article was an obvious entry point.

In the coming months, I analyzed countless pages of "talk page" discussions, reviewed hundreds of edits, and interviewed the editors of pages who would talk to me. I continued my investigation of the 2011 Egyptian revolution article for my PhD work at the Oxford Internet Institute between 2012 and 2015. One of my supervisors, Mark Graham, had developed the first representations of inequality on Wikipedia. He involved me in a project to study Wikipedia in the Middle East, funded by the Canadian International Development Research Centre. We went to Cairo and Aman and talked to Wikipedians about their challenges on wiki and their hopes for Wikipedia in the region.

It has been over a decade since I started studying this single article. The single most important thing that I learned over this time is the truly subversive role of Wikipedia. Jimmy Wales was right when he gave that prescient speech in Alexandria in 2008. Wikipedia tends to be ignored because it is supposedly "neutral." It is the only one of the world's most popular platforms that is maintained by a nonprofit organization. Its mirage of neutrality is sustained by the idea that individuals may be biased but all crowds are wise.

But no representation is truly neutral, and platforms, we have learned,[10] are certainly not. Rather than demonstrating how Wikipedia was losing its encyclopedic characteristics, as Dror Kamir had remarked, I argue in this book that the article about the 2011 Egyptian revolution shows how Wikipedia is leading a change to the form and nature of the encyclopedia itself. A primary catalyst of this change is Wikipedia's evolution as a data project. Wikipedia is increasingly a platform for the curation not of facts but of factual *data*. When that data is curated on an open platform *as events take place* (rather than after their import has stabilized), I argue, the result is an intense struggle over data and its meaning across multiple battlefronts where the classification of data is being decided. These struggles constitute a particular type of cyber warfare that is rarely discussed by cybersecurity think tanks. In 2011, it was data warfare conducted increasingly by online crowds and digital activists. Today, government agents and private public relations firms are added to the fray.

The year 2011 was when Wikipedia's subversive power came into its own. This book documents this moment in history and the decade that followed. It is a testament to a radical change that we are witnessing in what it means to know the world and who has the power to determine that knowledge.

In the end, I didn't find the argument that would break Wikipedia. Quite to the contrary, I recognized just how important Wikipedia is—but not for the reasons I once thought. Wikipedia is important not because of its uniqueness but because of its connections to the internet that we have built. Rather than a vision that is neutral and all-seeing, Wikipedia's vision is partial. Like all representational forms, Wikipedia is subject to both the machinations of people and their power struggles, and the affordances of the machines that are essential to its workings. This doesn't make Wikipedia bad. It just makes Wikipedia real. And seeing platforms for how they really shape the world is one of our most important priorities right now.

1

WIKIPEDIA MATTERS

In January 2018, Google mistakenly declared Vladimir Putin the winner of the upcoming Russian elections—two months early. This curious error was displayed in response to a Russian-language Google search for "elections 2018." The query resulted in a list of "facts" about the impending election in Google's featured "knowledge panel," a fact box on the right-hand side of Google's search results as pictured in figure 1.1 below.

The knowledge panel is an algorithmically generated list of information about people, places, events, things, and other entities. In this case, it included Putin's portrait under the heading "winner" in the knowledge panel about the election.

No source was available for the claim, but Google has indicated[1] that many of the "facts" in the knowledge panel are derived from Wikipedia. So the Russian press tracked down members of Wikimedia Russia[2] to explain the mishap. According to a spokesperson, a Wikipedia editor had added Putin's name to the preamble of the Russian Wikipedia article about the elections. Google's algorithms had indexed that claim and then reflected it in its knowledge panels.

The engine driving Google's knowledge panels is Google's knowledge graph—a database built from algorithms scouring the web for statements about people, places, events, and other entities. Google is not the only organization to have built a knowledge graph, and search engines are

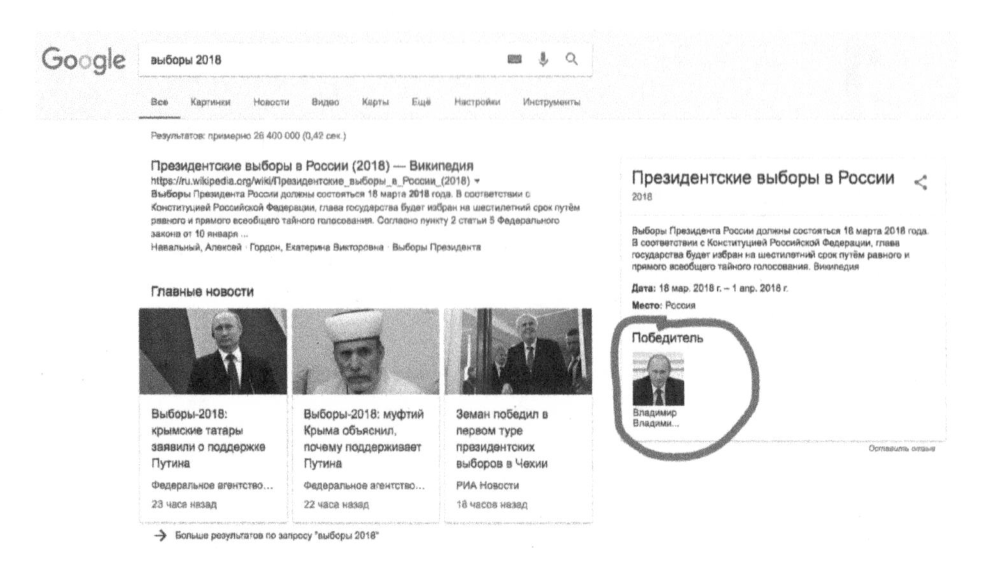

1.1 Screenshot of Putin result in Russian Google, January 14, 2018 (from Global Voices, January 16, 2018).

not their only application. Comprising billions of claims about people, places, events, things, and other entities automatically extracted from the web, knowledge graphs power information retrieval systems like Bing and Google Search as well as recommender systems and question-answering systems such as Google's Home, Apple's Siri, and Amazon's Alexa.

Knowledge graphs represent the future of knowledge discovery as search engines and voice assistants have been redesigned to encourage us to ask *questions* of our *devices* rather than *search for information* on *websites*. Before knowledge graphs, we searched for "Russian election results" and received a long list of websites providing information outside of the search engine (also called organic search), prioritized according to factors like the freshness of content and the number of other sites linking to it. Now, we can ask "Who won the 2018 Russian election?" and get a single answer directly inside the search engine.

In 2011, if you typed in "Who is Vladimir Putin?," Google would return a list of suggested websites according to keywords in the query. But after the knowledge graph was launched in 2012, it added what appeared to be a definitive answer to the query in the form of a fact box on the top right of the page: "Vladimir Putin: Russian President; Born: 7 October 1952;

Spouse: Lyudmila Aleksandrovna Ocheretnaya" and so on. (In figure 1.2 you can see a more recent screenshot of Google's answer to the question.) Critical to this change was an epistemological revolution: knowledge platforms are becoming a direct *source* of facts about the world, rather than a *directory* of knowledge sources.

The problem is that Google and other platforms that use knowledge graph technology don't curate answers entirely themselves. They use algorithms to select the "best" answer from the web's sources. "Best" is defined as the most relevant and highest-quality information. But quality is not determined by the claims' actual truth value (algorithms can't determine the truth). In addition to factors like the number of in-bound links, sources like Wikipedia and the Central Intelligence Agency (CIA) World Factbase[3] are prioritized by the algorithm, regardless of the "quality" of individual data points in a particular article or language version.

1.2 Screenshot of Google search results for "Who is Vladimir Putin?," September 2021.

Google isn't in the business of producing these claims itself (content development is difficult and resource-intensive). Instead, knowledge graphs like Google's are populated through a process of connecting factual claims from different sources about (what the algorithm recognizes is) the same entity. Google has always highlighted Wikipedia in its search rankings.[4] Wikipedia was ranked highly on Google because it is updated around the clock, boasts almost six million pages, and has been around for twenty years (significant in internet time), which has enabled a number of other sites to link to it. Wikipedia is even more useful to Google in the move toward an answer-based web. Now, Wikipedia's "infoboxes" are a ready source of openly licensed, datafied facts, organized according to a common semantic language that can be easily translated by the machines that operate search and discovery on digital platforms. This has turned Wikipedia into a prime source of datafied facts for Google and other third-party platforms because it produces statements organized according to standard formats that are easily recognized by algorithmic structures. But it isn't only Wikipedia's material structure that makes it authoritative. The ways in which truth is built—the grammars we use to perform authority—change over time. And Wikipedia's epistemology fits well with our current logics about truth and the procedures it is most likely to result from.

"Each society," wrote the French philosopher Michel Foucault, "has its regime of truth, its 'general politics' of truth: that is, the types of discourse which it accepts and makes function as true; the mechanisms and instances which enable one to distinguish true and false statements, the means by which each is sanctioned; the techniques and procedures accorded value in the acquisition of truth; the status of those who are charged with saying what counts as true."[5] Wikipedia's truth value is founded on the assumption that it does not participate in the messy business of truth telling, but merely reflects the truth "outside."

Wikipedia was founded on three core policies: neutral point of view (NPOV), no original research, and verifiability, with consensus being the main vehicle for editorial decision-making. The NPOV policy determines that Wikipedia's articles should explain all perspectives on a specific entity rather than taking "sides." According to this policy, Wikipedia manages to avoid entanglements with the truth because all material in Wikipedia must be attributed to "reliable sources" rather than editors' opinions.

Consensus is the main vehicle for achieving Wikipedia's neutrality and involves incorporating "all editors' legitimate concerns, while respecting Wikipedia's policies and guidelines."[6] The result is facts that seem to perfectly represent the world outside the platform in which they are produced.

The Putin error was corrected on Wikipedia after just twenty minutes, and within a few hours on Google. For both platforms, this was not a big deal: the mistake was quickly corrected, and no harm was done. Sometimes errors occur, but they are few and are quickly corrected. For others, however, this error wasn't so insignificant. Global Voices reporter Christopher Moldes wrote about Russian media and social media reaction to Google's error in an article titled "Why Wait? Wikipedia and Google Accidentally Declare Putin the Winner of March 2018 Presidential Elections."[7] Moldes reported that Alexey Pushkov, a Russian senator on the Council of the Russian Federation's Committee for Defense and Security, tweeted in response to the error: "Someone call Senator Pushkov. Using Google, the Americans have interfered in our elections, putting forth a candidate that will be favorable for them."

Although a clearly tongue-in-cheek response, the tweet demonstrates how much truth value is placed in Google's search results and the importance of Wikipedia in constructing the datafied facts that billions around the world rely on to govern their daily lives. Wikipedia presents itself as a neutral platform in which truth arises from the collective contributions of multiple voices (the so-called wisdom of crowds popularized by James Surowiecki[8]). If Wikipedia is biased, according to this logic, it is only so because the outside world has biased views. I call this "the mirror theory" of Wikipedia. According to this theory, Wikipedia can't be responsible for bias and inequality, because it merely mirrors the world's existing prejudices. If Wikipedia is biased against women and the Global South, according to this theory, it is because it is merely reflecting prejudice that already exists.

The mirror theory of Wikipedia assumes that Wikipedia is a neutral platform, that it doesn't participate in the world that it represents. The aim of this book is to demonstrate just how powerfully Wikipedia actively co-constructs the world it represents. In the context of an increasingly datafied web, I aim to show you just how powerfully Wikipedia is being shaped according to the logics, order, and demands of data.

I do this through a story about how the English Wikipedia article about the 2011 Egyptian revolution was created and how its classification was transformed from "protests" to "revolution." In the case of Wikipedia's recording of historic events as they unfold, Wikipedia co-constructs the event through the frame of its infrastructure. By creating a space in the database for a particular event, Wikipedia helps signify the event as nationally historic and important on the global stage. By classifying the event as an event of a particular kind (protest vs. revolution; war vs. genocide), Wikipedia helps determine international response to the event. By organizing facts according to rules that make them easily consumable by algorithms employed by search engines like Google, decisions made on Wikipedia about what counts as valid knowledge about an event and what constitutes "mere opinion" become globally significant. Rather than staying behind the curve of public opinion, Wikipedia is actively at its front.

As a result of this growing authority, Wikipedia is a major site of struggle in which power, rather than truth, often wins out. Catalyzed by historic events, crowds descend on Wikipedia to collate facts into a narrative account of what happened and why it happened. Control over facts can have significant political consequences, and so determining what those facts look like is often fiercely contested on Wikipedia. Data about events originating on Wikipedia is authoritative because it appears to emerge from a deliberative, rational space in which all voices come together to reach common consensus. Actually, Wikipedia's editing norms and logics result in decisions that are often achieved by force (of strategic editors and large crowds) rather than rational deliberation. Who and what win out in this battle (and what the consequences are) are the subjects of this book.

FACTS AND THEIR COMPANIONS

I've been talking a lot about facts, but what are facts? And how are they determined? It is important to remember that facts are not knowledge. Knowledge resides in the mind, in the body, and in the flow of practice between people living and working together. Facts, on the other hand, are material representations of knowledge: they are autonomous (they have meaning and can exist on their own); short (usually consisting of a subject, object, and qualifier); and specific (relating to a particular area of knowledge).[9]

You'll notice that the word "true" does not feature in my definition. Instead of defining facts as "true statements," I follow science and technology studies scholars by defining facts according to their materiality and symbolism rather than their essential truth value. We cannot begin our search for how truth is constructed on Wikipedia by attempting to determine the truth or falsity of a statement. Rather, it is more important to follow statements that are presented by their authors as representing objective reality in order to understand how that reality is constructed.

Many facts are stable (there is widespread consensus about their truth value). But there are facts that emerge as a result of catalytic events that are unstable and contentious when they first appear. Think about the first time that marriage was defined without regard to the gender of those marrying in the United States, that the World Health Organization categorized COVID-19 as a global pandemic, that Joe Biden was announced as the US president. In the wake of these transformative events, alternative claims jockey for priority in order to be accepted as the stable consensus.

In order for facts to become widely accepted, they need to travel from one community of practice to another. Facts are constructed locally, but they are constructed in order to travel. Few communities want their knowledge to stay hidden from the outside world, and so helping facts to travel is core business for knowledge industries like science, journalism, and encyclopedias. For facts to travel well, then, the methods by which they were constructed need to be accepted by the communities they travel to.

On the web, one of the most important destinations for facts is to be offered as the single answer to user questions in the prime position of the knowledge panel in search engines and as spoken by digital assistants as illustrated in figure 1.3 below. Determining the answer to the question "Who won the United States presidential election?" in Google's knowledge graph shortly after the voting period is an act of powerful political

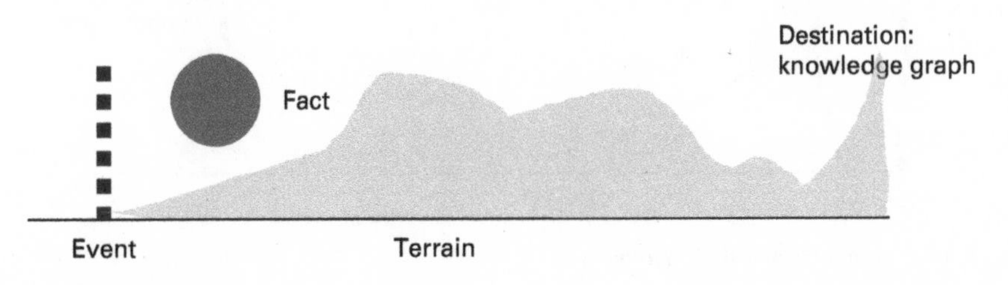

1.3 Digital facts.

construction. This final destination is challenging to arrive at, and there is intense competition to get there; but if facts can reach this prime position, they will reach billions of users.

In order to travel to such prime real estate, facts must be wrapped in metadata and exist in a format that knowledge graphs recognize. Datafied facts will travel farther through the infrastructure of the internet than facts that are merely expressed as HTML code. Data is rocket fuel for facts because it enables machines to recognize and extract facts that can later be represented as answers to user queries. Data constitutes a fact's labels and packaging that explain its meaning to machines and provides instructions on how it should be translated to other sites across the web as illustrated in figure 1.4 below.

In order for a fact to travel well as data, it also requires traveling "companions" and "allies"—particular individuals, groups, or institutions that help it in its travels. On Wikipedia, a fact's allies are its authors, the Wikipedia editors who add, remove, and change facts as they work in small groups and large crowds. A fact's allies also include nonhuman algorithms that automatically select a fact and extract or copy it across databases where it is represented in different contexts.

A fact's traveling companions (see figure 1.5) include the sources from which the fact (supposedly) originated. On Wikipedia, a fact's traveling companions are supposed to be visible and transparent to the reader. Google does not share Wikipedia's requirement that all material must be attributable to reliable, published sources (as we saw in the example in the beginning of this chapter). Facts' traveling companions are often discarded along the way.

The truth of facts is constructed in practice according to rules, logics, and cultures of a society, profession, or community. These forces constitute

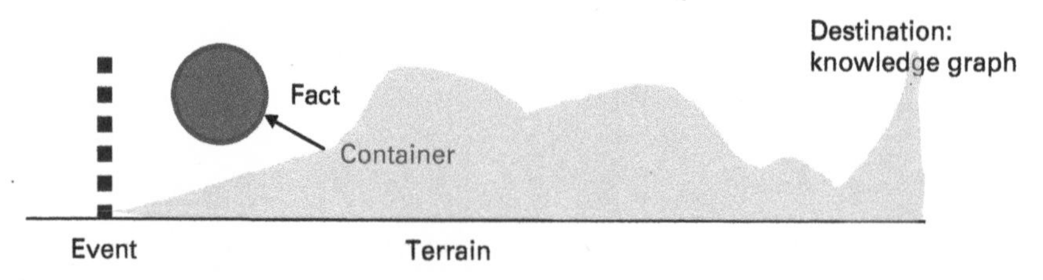

1.4 Digital facts and their containers.

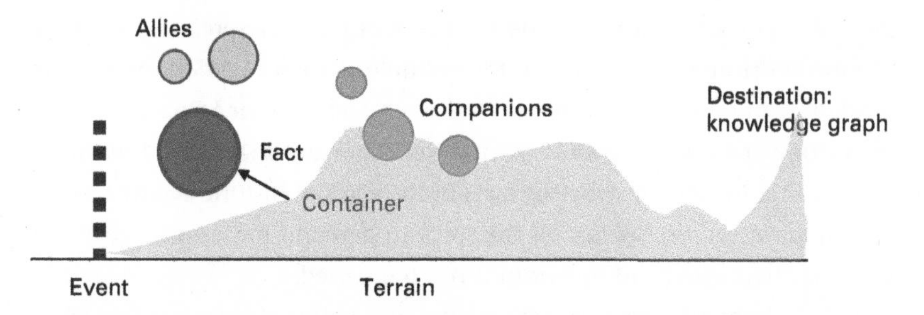

1.5 Digital facts and their allies and companions.

the "terrain" or infrastructure in which facts travel. Infrastructure is both social and technical. It is made up of social features: the rules, policies, and social norms that guide the creation of facts and their translation across different sites. It is also constituted by software code that makes up the machinery, defining how facts are created as data and how malleable they are to which actors.

Infrastructure stretches across multiple platforms, and the terrain changes as facts move through different platforms. Although they share exchange protocols that ensure facts can travel between them, the terrain of each platform is either rocky or smooth for the facts that travel along it. Rules and practices guide decisions in communities of knowledge practice about what constitutes valid knowledge.

In the wake of historic events, the demand for facts reaches a fever pitch. As the scholar of events Robin Wagner-Pacifici writes, unexpected events like the September 11 attacks seem to descend on us from out of the blue, causing an information vacuum and a corresponding need by the public for information in order to alleviate the sense of dis-ease that necessarily follows.[10] Something happens (a bomb detonates in a crowded park, a masked gunman fires shots in the street, catastrophic fires decimate whole towns), and it rocks our previous understandings of the world. Out of the sense of "dis-ease and incomprehension" we try to find those who are responsible for rupturing our social fabric, to locate where events originate, however premature that is. We ask questions about what is happening and to whom it is happening.

In response, knowledge agents construct factual claims about events and, in doing so, symbolically ascribe the identities of legitimate witnesses, victims, and perpetrators. At the time of writing, widespread protests are occurring throughout Myanmar, for example. A total of 745 protesters are dead, and the junta are to blame. Although facts appear to exist on their own, they are always "about" something. They are meaningful within a particular context. Constructing facts in the wake of historic events attracts enormous attention because of the spike in demand for knowledge about what has happened and to whom it has happened.

I've described forces that are internal and external to any single community of practice producing facts about the world. Facts on Wikipedia, for example, are constructed by the fact's allies (or authors) and shaped by the companions (sources) that are selected by its allies to authorize it. Facts are wrapped in labels (metadata) that describe the fact for machines that translate that fact across sites. External forces are significant here too. They include the market for sources available outside of Wikipedia, the attention of readers and potential editors channeled from third-party platforms like Google, and metadata models developed by web communities that provide labeling standards. Facts are ultimately also influenced by the event itself, which seems to descend on the world from out of the blue and leads to a spike in demand for facts about what has happened.

This is why I argue that Wikipedia *co*-constructs the world. Both internal and external forces are ultimately responsible for the facts that Wikipedia produces. Wikipedia does not exist as an island on its own. It responds to the volatility of historic events and is indelibly connected to an increasingly commercial web built by corporate behemoths loyal only to their shareholders.

Why does this matter for Wikipedia? What's at stake?

HOW WIKIPEDIA SHAPES THE WORLD

Wikipedia's goal is to "[provide] every single person on the planet [with] access to the sum of all human knowledge."[11] Unlike the majority of content on the internet today, Wikipedia is free for anyone to edit, copy, and share its contents. It is licensed under a Creative Commons Attribution Share-Alike copyright license, which provides up-front permission for these uses, potentially enabling anyone to copy Wikipedia's entire contents and republish it on a different site, provided they attribute Wikipedia as the source and apply the same license to the new contents.

Wikipedia bills itself as the encyclopedia that anyone can edit. It is one of the most popular websites on the planet and the only website in the top fifteen that is hosted by a nonprofit organization. Wikipedia is also the biggest encyclopedia, consisting of more than forty million encyclopedic articles developed and maintained by thousands of volunteers from around the world and available in more than three hundred languages. It has no commercial ads and is open to anyone with the time, interest, and tenacity to contribute.

Wikipedia appears as a utopia in which everyone's knowledge can eventually be represented. But the site suffers from significant systemic biases. Only about 20 percent of Wikipedia's 6.2 million biographies are of women,[12] about 85 percent of Wikipedia editors are male, and topics with a female audience are weakly represented.[13]

There are also significant geographical imbalances to Wikipedia's coverage. Wikipedia's articles, topics, and contributors are more likely to represent the United States and Western Europe with large parts of the developing world underrepresented. In 2014, for example, my supervisor at the Oxford Internet Institute, Mark Graham, and colleagues found that only about 1 percent of edits originate from Africa and that countries, cities, and towns in Africa are significantly underrepresented.[14] More recently, research has demonstrated the multiple vectors of bias—including the ways in which topics are positioned, characterized, and represented on Wikipedia.[15]

Despite this wealth of research outlining Wikipedia's limited scope, our understanding of the reasons for Wikipedia's partiality is still lacking. In 2018, for example, when Donna Strickland won the Nobel Prize for physics, it was discovered that she had been previously denied a Wikipedia page because editors believed that she had not been notable enough. The response—by both the media and Wikipedia—demonstrated that there is still widespread misunderstanding about Wikipedia's role in shaping the world.

Journalists in the United States wrote a number of stories decrying Wikipedia's culture and pointing to its tiny proportion of female editors and biographies (pages) after Strickland's win. In response, the Wikimedia

Foundation's director at the time, Katherine Maher, wrote on Twitter: "Journalists—if you're going to come after @Wikipedia for its coverage of women, check your own coverage first. We're a mirror of the world's biases, not the source of them. We can't write articles about what you don't cover" (@krmaher, October 3, 2018).

What Maher reflected in this tweet was one of the dominant theories held by Wikipedians, even those working to fill the site's content gaps: the mirror theory that I mentioned earlier. One of Wikipedia's core content policies is that its article must be developed out of what Wikipedia and Wikipedians consider "reliable sources." Since Wikipedia can only cover topics written about in reliable sources, the theory goes, it is dependent on what those sources cover. For this reason, Wikipedia overrepresents male scientists rather than female scientists and towns in the Global North versus those in the Global South.

The mirror theory assumes that Wikipedia's biases originate from outside Wikipedia: that Wikipedia reflects the world unequally in the same way that the world's knowledge sources are unequally represented. Patterns in the unequal representation of female scientists, for example, emulate traditional patterns of gender bias; representations of people, places, and events in the Global South echo skews in the inequalities that riddle the publishing industry and that mirror the digital divide.

The problem with the mirror theory is that it assumes that Wikipedia is a neutral platform that doesn't participate in the world it passively summarizes. It doesn't account for anomalies to Wikipedia's perfect mirroring of traditional inequalities in publishing power, like those of academic and newspaper publishing. For example, Wikipedia doesn't perfectly represent the biases of traditional knowledge sources when it overrepresents digital cultures and topics that are well represented on the internet and underrepresents topics and languages not well represented online. Or when it overrepresents current history (well represented in online platforms) rather than events from the distant past (which tend not to be digitized).

Wikipedia also results in anomalies at the level of language. Cebuano, for example, is a language spoken only in the southern Philippines. But Cebuano Wikipedia is the second-biggest language edition of Wikipedia. Although it is a tiny language in relation to the number of people who speak it, its size is largely due to bots administered by only a handful of editors that have automatically translated articles from English (and other large language Wikipedias) into Cebuano. The ways in which Wikipedia embraces automated means of knowledge production have resulted in a refracturing of the position of Cebuano in terms of other global languages. This has also resulted in significant embarrassment by Philippine Wikipedians because their encyclopedia doesn't reflect local knowledge or interest.[16]

The mirror theory also doesn't account for Wikipedia's connection to the web on which it depends and that crucially depends on *it*. As the opening story of this chapter suggests, the facts that Wikipedia produces and that circulate through the web are subject to multiple forces, both inside and outside Wikipedia. When Google pronounced Vladimir Putin the winner of the election before it even happened, the untrustworthy fact was found to have originated in an edit by a single Wikipedia editor and then reinscribed by Google's algorithms. When Donna Strickland eventually got a Wikipedia page (which was also indexed by Google and inscribed in the knowledge graph), that page was determined by the Wikipedia editors who produced it and by the sources outside of Wikipedia that were cited in the article. And in both of these examples it was the event itself (an election, an award announcement) that catalyzed a reconfiguration in the representation of Putin and Strickland.

In the Donna Strickland affair, Wikimedia's Katherine Maher soon recognized her mistake and responded with a series of tweets acknowledging Wikipedia's internal biases. "I criticized institutions for their biases and underplayed the production bias inherent in our own. That was hasty and reductionist. I was intending to respond to a specific article instance but failed to lay the groundwork acknowledging our own systemic challenges" (@krmaher, October 3, 2018). It was an easy mistake. The "Wikipedia as a mirror" theory is still the dominant way of framing Wikipedia's role in knowledge production.

I started my research career trying to understand Wikipedia's biases. But when I began researching Wikipedia's articles about current events, I became interested in looking beyond bias to the ways in which Wikipedia is shaped by and in turn shapes the world. This approach requires understanding both the internal and external forces that influence who and what have influence over Wikipedia's representations.

Wikipedia is usually recognized as an exception to the platform capitalism that the world's most powerful companies have been identified with. It is "the last best place on the internet,"[17] the only nonprofit platform in a sea of corporate behemoths that have degraded our democracies. And yet, Wikipedia is connected in indelible ways to the logics of other major platforms. Like Google, Wikipedia plays a dominating role in our information ecosystems. *Not* being represented on these platforms is a death knell for facts and the people they represent.

I argue that Wikipedia is no longer just an encyclopedia. Like Google, Wikipedia constitutes critical knowledge infrastructure. Like electricity grids, telephone and sewerage networks, platforms including Wikipedia and Google provide knowledge infrastructure that millions of people around the world depend on to make decisions in everyday life. Despite their importance, we are usually unaware of the workings of our knowledge infrastructure until it breaks down. When that happens, we get a glimpse not only of how platforms share data between one another but also the attempts of people trying to influence their representations.

Because of Wikipedia's status not only as an encyclopedia, as one representation among many, but also as the infrastructure for the production and travel of facts, the ways in which decisions are made about which descriptions, explanations, and classifications are selected over others become critical. Wikipedia is authoritative because it seems to reflect what is the consensus truth about the world. How, then, is so-called consensus arrived at? Who (or what) wins in these struggles? What does it take to win? How do battles play out across the chains of circulation in which datafied facts now travel? Does this ultimately represent a people's history, reflective of our global collective intelligence? Is history now written by algorithms, or do certain groups and actors actually dominate that representation?

These are the questions that the book seeks to answer. Journalists may write the first draft of history, and historians document expert accounts by revisiting those sources after events have occurred. But on Wikipedia, accounts of historic events are being created in ways that are more powerful and more popular than any single authoritative source. Rather than representing global consensus, the facts that are curated and circulated through the web's most trusted terrains are the result of significant struggles and the constant discarding of alternatives. Some actors and technologies prevail in this struggle, while other knowledges are either actively rejected or never visible from the start.

SHAPING HISTORY-IN-THE-MAKING

The best illustration of how Wikipedia shapes the world, I have learned, is in its representation of current events—articles about both the events themselves and the subjects that become embroiled in those events. This includes articles in which the event itself is the focus—for example, articles connected to the 2019–2020 Australian bushfires and those that received significant boosts in editing, including climate change, Scott Morrison (the Australian prime minister at the time), and koalas.

If you go to English Wikipedia right now (as in 2022), you'll notice an "In the news" section in the top right-hand corner of the page. Headlines of important international events are listed there, some with keywords linked to Wikipedia articles (biographies of politicians, for example), while others are linked to articles about recent events. Emergencies such as the COVID-19 global pandemic, as well as armed conflicts, terrorist attacks, disasters, and accidents, are covered by Wikipedians in great detail, usually just a matter of minutes or hours after a bomb goes off, a shot is fired, or an earthquake strikes.

Wikipedia's articles about current events are among the most widely read historical accounts and the sources of data about events that become lodged in our current truth machines. The article "Killing of George Floyd" on June 6, 2020, for example, attracted almost ten million views in the two weeks after the event.[18] Wikipedia's articles relating to breaking news topics are actually the most popular to read and write about.[19] About two hundred million readers visit Wikipedia every day, but this doesn't count the billions who encounter Wikipedia's content via search engines and intelligent agents that answer users' questions about the world using Wikipedia data.

Media events scholar Paddy Scannell wrote in 1995 that it was impossible for events to "have any public meaning without their transmission by (television) broadcasting."[20] Today, because of our growing reliance on data, it is becoming impossible for events to have any public meaning without their transmission as data. Although the Wikipedia article about the Egyptian revolution of 2011 is now a few thousand-word retelling of events as they happened, the most important information that Wikipedians curate is data about the event. Event data includes facts about the event (What kind of event? How many dead? Who were the belligerents?) wrapped in labels that translate their meaning for the machines that transport and display them.

Given Wikipedia's strategic location, who is best able to influence such representations? Wikipedia is open to editing by all, but this doesn't mean that anyone could write anything about the protests that erupted in Egypt in early 2011. What defines Wikipedia's scope of participation is not its open content license that invites anyone to edit. Rather, it is the platform's architecture, the organization of which shapes participation.

In the case of the historic events in Egypt in early 2011, activist editors co-constructed the event by first carving a space into Wikipedia's database with the creation of a new article. They coordinated their activities with other editors in order to stabilize their representation of the event, its meaning and significance. They defended their representation by rooting it into the fabric of the web by connecting facts to their companions (sources).

Editors used the materials at their disposal on Wikipedia to create and package datafied facts that would be easily transported to other platforms. But editors were not free to create just *any* representations on Wikipedia. In tracing the travel of facts as they are first formed, developed, altered, and translated over the course of a rapidly evolving historic event, two other forces emerge as critical in writing the revolution into being.

The first is the crowd—groups of inexperienced editors who descend on the site to influence its representations on the back of waves of media attention. The crowd emerges at key stages because of the second key force: the event itself. The protests that bubbled up in Tahrir Square, Cairo, and greater Egypt resulted in an information vacuum and a corresponding need for publics to seek information in order to ease the sense of dis-ease that always follows the start of unplanned events. This vacuum drove editing activity on Wikipedia and catalyzed the production of myriad sources from journalistic and other institutions representing the event outside of Wikipedia.

After facts have been established on Wikipedia, they are subject to another coup d'état that further limits the power of Wikipedians. This time it is by the algorithmic apparatus of the knowledge graph, imposed on the article from afar. When the knowledge graph is operated by Google, facts are extracted from Wikipedia's domain and re-presented within the walled gardens of the proprietary platform, where new rules for public engagement dominate. When the knowledge graph is operated by Wikidata, a sister project of Wikipedia, control is ceded to algorithms and their operators.

Data about events originating on Wikipedia is authoritative because it appears to emerge from a deliberative, rational space in which all voices come together to reach common consensus. However, the article that was written about events as they unfolded in Egypt was inhabited by passion and feverish anticipation of revolution from its very first version, just hours after the protests began on January 25. Rather than rational consensus among dispassionate observers, Wikipedia mirrored the passion, emotion, and violence of Tahrir Square.

In the decade after the revolution, facts about the event were subject to yet another power wrangling—this time over the jurisdiction and governance of facts under the control of those who originally formulated them. Algorithmic actors like the Google knowledge graph appear to dispassionately and independently adjudicate which of the multitude of alternative classifications are the most reliable from around the web. Actually, the knowledge graph actively participates in mediating data representations by prioritizing particular sources (including Wikipedia) and by representing facts, often with changed meaning, according to its own logics. Facts curated by the graph are never a perfect mirror of their source, and the graph prioritizes statements not because they are more truthful (algorithms cannot adjudicate the truth) but because they fit neatly into the material form of the knowledge graph and because Wikipedia appears to represent the consensus view.

Looking at the recording of historic events as they happen on Wikipedia demonstrates that, rather than mirroring external representations in journalistic accounts, Wikipedia is at the front line of data wars being fought using novel weapons and tactics. Articles about political events are important battlegrounds for multiple interest groups from around the world who are vying for control over the historical record on Wikipedia. Far from a reflection of the neutral point of view, the consensus truth about what happened, Wikipedia's representations are the result of a struggle in which power rather than truth sometimes wins, and the key battlefronts are where its facts are being translated into data.

Studying Wikipedia's articles about current events offers immediate and powerful evidence of the ways in which decisions on Wikipedia affect what many people around the world accept as historical fact.

WRITING THE REVOLUTION

Most of us are probably aware that a revolution occurred in Egypt in 2011. If one asks Google what happened in Egypt in 2011, it will provide a list of facts about "the Egyptian revolution of 2011" and perhaps even show the source from Wikipedia. That events in Egypt in early 2011 constituted a revolution is settled. It has reached consensus. It appears to be stable, indisputable knowledge, according to public understanding and consensus. But this wasn't always so. Many alternative descriptions and explanations competed on the global stage as events played out in the streets of Egypt's cities and in the famous Tahrir Square.

Understanding how the 2011 Egyptian revolution was co-constructed by Wikipedia is important, not least because of its significance in terms of Egyptian history and politics but because of its significance in the history of the web. In the wake of protests that culminated in what came to be known as the Arab Spring, *Time* magazine labeled 2011 "the year of the protester." The Egyptian revolution, in particular, was a pivotal moment for drawing attention to the role of digital technology in shaping politics.

The Egyptian revolution was televised live, like many of the historic protests of the latter part of the last century and those that have erupted since 2011, such as the Black Lives Matter protests in the United States following the death of George Floyd in 2020. Television networks played a critical role in signifying the importance and scale of the events in Egypt, as the aerial camera views pictured hundreds of thousands of people amassing on Tahrir Square in Cairo. But the television media did not monopolize the coverage of events in Egypt.

Before the first television broadcasts of the protests reached the international public, the event was fomented by thousands of Egyptians on social media. This was the first major event to foreground the role of platforms in enabling social and political dissent and where the role of platforms has been heavily debated since. Some nominated technology as the lead actor in driving these events forward.

There are now a host of articulate accounts of how Facebook and Twitter proved instrumental for activists as an organizing tool for the daily protests that culminated in Hosni Mubarak's resignation. Jared Cohen cited an Egyptian activist summing up the roles of social media in the revolution: "facebook used to set the date, twitter used to share logistics, youtube to show the world, all to connect people."[21]

In his excellent book *Tweets and the Streets*, Paolo Gerbaudo argues that the role of social media in the wave of social movements that took place in the early part of this century is much more expansive than the technical operations that quotes like this suggest. Neither does social media result in "unrestrained participation" by all. Instead, social media enabled activists to choreograph collective action. Platforms like Twitter, Facebook, and YouTube enabled the symbolic construction of public space in which influential online activists could become "choreographers." Not all individuals had equal agency to effect change. Influential activists used social media for "setting the scene, and constructing an emotional space within which collective action (could) unfold."[22]

But what of Wikipedia? A decade after the revolution, Wikipedia's representations of the event are more popular and certainly more enduring than any other source. Wikipedia is the origin of the event's factual classification in the most popular re-presentations of the event. Instead of enabling the coordination of action on the ground during the protests, Wikipedia facilitated the narration of events in the enduring form of the encyclopedia as events unfolded. And yet I have found only a single early study examining Wikipedia's role in the Egyptian revolution.[23]

The majority of scholars who have studied Wikipedia's role in history making and knowledge construction have tended to accept that Wikipedia articles are the result of consensus. According to this research, Wikipedia is "a global memory place"[24] that is able to reflect "common knowledge"[25] and "collective memory."[26]

But this view of Wikipedia's role does not address the problem that there are always multiple versions of events when they first occur and that these must be organized into a single account. There are manifold ways of knowing the world and narrating history, and there are always winners and losers in any single account. I follow the editors, sources, automated tools, algorithms, and crowds over the course of a decade in the life of the English Wikipedia article about the revolution in order to understand who wins in this environment. What becomes clear is that Wikipedia may produce a shared experience among those editors in particular language editions who worked together during the greatest peak in the article's popularity. But representation on Wikipedia at any one moment is reflective not of agreement but sometimes of surrender in the face of stronger forces.

My research for this book is the result of a decade-long multisited ethnographic study.[27] It reflects my following of factual claims about the 2011 Egyptian revolution from when they were first embedded in a Wikipedia article within hours of the first protests in Egypt across a decade.

Ethnographies typically focus on a single site, and multisited ethnography involves following people or things as they travel through global systems. In *Writing the Revolution* I move between locations on the ground and locations in digital infrastructures in order to understand how protests played out across different locales. Beginning on the streets of Cairo, where the editor of the first version of the English Wikipedia article about the protests was located, I traverse locations in the United States, the United Arab Emirates, the United Kingdom (UK), Germany, and a number of other countries around the world.

A few of the interviews were conducted face-to-face, mostly at Wikipedia conferences, including at the start of my PhD when I helped facilitate workshops involving Wikipedians from the Middle East in Egypt and Jordan. But the majority were conducted using videoconferencing software and online chat, with follow-ups often taking place over email.

In the pages that follow, I trace five stages in which facts about historic events travel through Wikipedia and out to the wider web: genesis, eruption, escalation, surge, and translation. Each represents a key moment in which events are classified according to data and in which those classifications travel to the wider web.

In researching this book, I had a glimpse of the materiality of history in the age of automation: how stories about what happened in the world start off as malleable, peopled, available for transformation. But these stories are rapidly closed to debate and politics, often as a result of automated actions and the actions of crowds who, enlivened by emotion, are able to change the fate of nations. Wikipedia is both emblematic of this change and a vehicle through which it is enabled.

2

GENESIS

On December 17, 2010, a twenty-six-year-old street vendor stood outside the governor's office in the town of Sidi Bouzid, 300 kilometers (190 miles) south of Tunisia's capital. Exasperated and humiliated, feeling powerless beyond measure, he set himself alight, shouting, "How do you expect me to make a living?" The man was Mohamed Bouazizi, and his self-immolation catalyzed the Arab Spring.

Bouazizi's words were intended for the municipal officials who harassed him earlier in the day (allegedly for not having a vendor's permit). After an official confiscated his weighing scales and tossed aside his cart, Bouazizi went to the governor's office to complain about his ill treatment, threatening to set himself on fire if he wasn't granted an appointment. When the governor refused to see him, Mohamed Bouazizi doused himself with a can of gasoline and set himself on fire in the middle of traffic.

After receiving a phone call about Bouazizi, Ali Bouazizi (a distant cousin of Mohamed's) arrived at the governor's office just in time to see Bouazizi ablaze. He captured the burning body (and the protest that followed) on his mobile phone camera and distributed it to local independent journalists.

In Qatar, Al Jazeera was receiving notifications about the incident, but the news organization was officially banned in Tunisia so it could not send its journalists there. Footage, images, and reports had been making their way to Al Jazeera via its recently launched citizen journalism portal, Sharek. Just hours after the incident, Ali Bouazizi's video (and an interview with him) aired on Al Jazeera Mubasher, a twenty-four-hour live news and events channel similar to CSPAN and BBC Parliament.

Communication and media studies scholar Merlyna Lim found that it was the event's framing rather than Bouazizi's death itself that propelled it into a large-scale movement.[1] Unlike other self-immolations, Bouazizi's burning body was captured on camera, elevating it to a public spectacle and reinforcing the injustice of his story. Ali Bouazizi told the media that his cousin Mohamed was an unemployed university graduate who turned to selling produce to make ends meet and that a female municipal official slapped him in the face during their altercation. Lim wrote that a slap from a woman to a man is seen as particularly humiliating in Arab cultures and that this would have multiplied the anger of the conservative population. In reality, Bouazizi never finished high school, and nobody knew whether the slap really happened.

"By adding these two ingredients—a university graduate and a slap—to the story, Ali rendered Mohamed's burning body political, affixing to it the political body of a citizen whose rights were denied," writes Lim. "Mohamed Bouazizi no longer represented the uneducated poor who struggle to provide food on the table, but represented all young people of Tunisia whose rights and freedom were denied."[2]

These ingredients catapulted the story into public attention. Images and videos were uploaded to YouTube, shared on Facebook, and tweeted on Twitter. Starting with distribution by mobile phones and alternative media, Bouazizi's immolation was soon featured in traditional news broadcasts nationally and internationally.

Mohamed Bouazizi died in the hospital on January 4, 2011. A five-thousand-strong crowd marched in his funeral procession, chanting that they would avenge his death. Bouazizi was seen as a victim of the state's brutality: the story of his inability to survive in a society deaf to his struggles, and a government whose constant harassment compounded those struggles, provoked widespread anger. This story echoed through neighboring countries, where it inspired others to turn on their governments as the source of their woes. The framing of the protest narrative was critical to the success of protest movements, as we will soon learn was the case in Egypt as well.

On January 14, 2011, Tunisian president Zine El Abidine Ben Ali fled to Saudi Arabia, ending his twenty-six-year rule. Protests erupted in Algeria with one question hanging in the air: Who would be next? But in the days after Ben Ali's resignation, Western journalists based in Cairo wrote about life continuing as normal, with no major protests and no visible extra security.

A January 17 article for the BBC by Jon Leyne stated that there was "no sign Egypt will take the Tunisian road,"[3] despite the fact that Egypt was experiencing problems similar to those of Tunisia: rising food prices, tough economic conditions, widespread corruption, and little opportunity for people to voice their political concerns. After interviewing members of the opposition and people in the streets, Leyne concluded, "The simple fact is that most Egyptians do not see any way that they can change their country or their lives through political action, be it voting, activism, or going out on the streets to demonstrate."

On January 20, *Time* magazine echoed these sentiments. In an article headlined "Why Egypt Isn't Ready to Have Its Own Revolution," the Cairo-based journalist explained that, unlike Tunisia, Egypt's government had allowed spending on education to decay, preventing the establishment of a similar educated but unemployed population, which was key to Tunisia's revolt. Another factor was Egypt's armed forces. Whereas in Tunisia, "at a critical turning point, the Army took the side of the protesters," in Egypt, "the military stands with Mubarak."[4]

While Western journalists were commenting on Egyptians' apparent inability to take advantage of the Tunisian revolution, powerful narratives about injustice closer to home were setting the Egyptian social media sphere ablaze. One nucleus of that discontent was a Facebook memorial page called "Kullena Khaled Said" (We Are All Khaled Said). Khaled Mohamed Saeed (or Said) is the figure that looms large in the story of the Egyptian revolution and, indeed, in the story of how its history was written on Wikipedia. As Mohamed Bouazizi catalyzed the story of the Tunisian revolution, so too did Khaled Saeed in Egypt.

Saeed, who police said was wanted for theft and weapons possession, died in police custody on June 6, 2010, in Alexandria. Egyptian police reported that he suffocated when he swallowed a packet of hashish. His family said that he was, in fact, beaten to death by police because he possessed video material that implicated officers in a drug deal.

When Saeed's family visited his body in the morgue, his brother snapped pictures of the corpse using his mobile phone. The photo of Saeed's battered and deformed face went viral. A few days after his death, Wael Ghonim, an Egyptian Google marketing executive, created the Facebook memorial page for Saeed. Ghonim identified with Saeed and was shocked by the images of him. Talking about the events in a later interview with National Public Radio's Terry Gross, he recalled, "Looking at Khaled's photo after his death, basically, I just felt that we are all Khaled Said. That was a feeling. It wasn't just a brand name. It was a feeling. We were all of these young Egyptians who could die, and no one [would be] held accountable. So at the time, I thought, 'I have to do something.' And I believed that bringing Khaled's case to a public case would be helpful."[5]

The Facebook page attracted hundreds of thousands of followers, many of whom adopted Saeed's photograph for their own Facebook profiles. Many young Egyptians saw themselves in Saeed: a young person who had tried to stand up for justice but who had been violently murdered by a corrupt state that was unaccountable to its citizens.

Ghonim's Facebook page became a hub for discussion and dissent. On the day that Ben Ali left Tunisia, Ghonim wrote, "Today is the 14th of January. In 10 days, we have a police day. If 100,000 of us take to the street, no one is going to stop us."[6] Two hours later, Ghonim created an event titled "25 يناير على التعذيب والفساد والظلم والبطالة" (January 25: Revolution against torture, corruption, unemployment, and injustice).

National Police Day is a national holiday in Egypt that commemorates the deaths of fifty police officers who were killed when they refused British demands to hand over their weapons and evacuate a local police station in 1952. A week before the national public holiday, twenty-six-year-old activist Asmaa Mahfouz posted a video blog urging the Egyptian people to join her on January 25 in Cairo's Tahrir Square. The video went viral in Egypt and around the world after she uploaded it to YouTube and shared it on her Facebook page.[7]

"Whoever says women shouldn't go to the protests because they will get beaten, let him have some honor and manhood and come with me on

January 25th," she says in the video. "They don't even have to go to Tahrir Square, just go anywhere and say it: that we are free human beings."[8]

She warned people against simply watching from the sidelines. "Sitting home and just following us on news or on Facebook leads to our humiliation—it leads to *my humiliation!*" she says in the video. "If you have honor and dignity as a man, come and protect me, and other girls in the protest. If you stay home, you deserve what's being done to you, and you will be guilty before your nation and your people. Go down to the street, send SMSes, post it on the internet, make people aware."[9]

Tens of thousands signed up on Facebook to attend the event. Narratives about injustice, pride, honor, and emancipation were powerful—at least to the nation's educated youth. But protest organizers were unsure whether those who had signed up would actually show up. Had the frames worked? Would they be recognized by the Egyptian public?

ON WIKIPEDIA: FIRST FRAMER

The Egyptian Liberal is the Wikipedia username of the founding editor of the first article to cover the Egyptian protests in 2011. He was the first to frame events in Egypt for English Wikipedia's editor and reader communities and one of our facts' greatest allies. I spoke to The Egyptian Liberal for the first time in October 2012. We talked over Skype: he was in Dubai; I was in Oxford. I was about to go to Cairo to help facilitate a workshop with Wikipedians from the region. We talked about mutual friends. His voice was youthful, insistent.

A university student in his twenties, The Egyptian Liberal is Egyptian by birth but had been living elsewhere in the Middle East for most of his life. He returned to Egypt regularly for vacations and was actively involved in Egyptian politics. In addition to editing Wikipedia articles about soccer and television, he edited articles about politics in Egypt and the Middle East. He told me that he started editing Wikipedia because he wanted to correct inaccurate information about the Arab people.

The Egyptian Liberal is a Wikipedian, but his profile is rare among this group. Demographic studies of Wikipedia editors indicate that they are not representative of the world's population. Facebook and Twitter have more or less equal numbers of female and male users, but between 84 and 90 percent of Wikipedia editors are men,[10] the majority have tertiary education, and a significant number of editors across Wikipedia's 314 language versions speak English. According to a 2011 Wikimedia Foundation survey, 36 percent of the Wikipedia editor population can write computer programs. Although this isn't a dominant proportion, it is high in relation to the general population and reflects the technical nature of the community.[11]

The majority of Wikipedia's editors reside in the United States, followed by Germany and Russia.[12] Interestingly, the only country not in Europe or North America in the top ten locations for editing is India, and only about 1 percent of edits originate from Africa. Almost half of India's 1.37 billion population has access to the internet, placing it second in the world in terms of active internet users.

Wikipedia is concentrated in particular language versions, topics, and user demographics that frame our experience of the site and determine its politics. The majority of editors congregate on English Wikipedia, which is the largest and most active version, with over six million articles and almost forty thousand active editors. As a comparison, one of the smallest versions, Bambara Wikipedia (a West African language), had fewer than a thousand articles and about fifty active editors at the time of writing.[13]

English Wikipedia is the most populous in terms of readers, too. English Wikipedia accounts for almost 60 percent of Wikipedia's cumulative traffic, with the remaining split among the other languages. Even within English Wikipedia there are skews, and some topics tend to be much more crowded than others. The most popular articles tend to be those related to breaking news events on English Wikipedia. The majority of articles and topics are more likely to represent the United States and Western Europe, with large parts of the developing world underrepresented.

Editing a particular Wikipedia language edition does not necessarily reflect one's native language. It is estimated that about half of English Wikipedia editors are not native English speakers. Early on in Wikipedia's history, Wikipedia's cofounder Jimmy Wales urged editors to write articles in their own languages from scratch, rather than through translation.

When I helped organize the first African edit-a-thon for Wikipedia at the CIDA City Campus in Johannesburg in 2007, both Jimmy Wales and Ndesanjo Macha (a Swahili Wikipedian) talked about the importance of editing Wikipedia in one's own language.[14] Edit-a-thons are workshops where editors of online communities gather to learn how to edit and improve content related to a specific topic. The opportunity to edit Wikipedia in one's own language is a significant advancement on the encyclopedias of old. Encyclopedias before Wikipedia had been instruments of colonialism, objects of domination in which the knowledge of a single group was used to educate and subjugate another. The potential to create encyclopedias in local languages as a reflection of indigenous knowledges seemed like a significant achievement.

But Wikipedia is not neatly separable into different language versions where the language speakers of a particular country or region are free to represent their own perspectives on topics. A 2011 survey indicated that more than half of Wikipedia editors contribute to more than one language Wikipedia, and an overwhelming majority (72 percent) read Wikipedia in more than one language.[15] In a study led by the Wikipedia researcher Shilad Sen,[16] which I coauthored, we found that countries with large economies were extensively represented by editors who were local to that country, using local sources. But the majority of information about Africa and the Middle East was produced by editors and sources outside those regions.

The term "Wikipedian" identifies experienced editors who distinguish themselves from newcomers. Wikipedia's newcomers are marked by their lack of user pages, their inability to use the policy language of Wikipedia, and their low edit count. Experienced Wikipedians' user pages, on the other hand, tend to contain detailed information about their interests and philosophies of work, as well as strings of barnstars, awards that are given to editors by their peers for a job well done in a particular area of work.

Yet another class of Wikipedia editor (often from within the newcomer group) is the unregistered or anonymous user. Unregistered editors are those who don't register an account on Wikipedia. The term "anonymous" is somewhat of a misnomer since editors who don't log in are identified by their IP addresses, which can be looked up to discover the geolocation of the editor. This means that unregistered editors are in some ways less anonymous than those who are logged in since their location is public, whereas the IP addresses of registered users are hidden.

When people working from government computers edit Wikipedia as unregistered users, for example, Twitter bots automatically record the article they have edited and the location of the edit so that the public can check whether the edit was legitimate. The first WikiEdits bot, @ParliamentEdits, was created by British internet celebrity Tom Scott in 2014 to notify Twitter users every time an edit to Wikipedia was made from a British Parliamentary IP address. Since then, bots have been created for a host of other countries' governments, from the United States (@congressedits) to Australia (@AussieParlEdits), for corporations such as Goldman Sachs (@goldmanedits) and the IP addresses of oil and defense contractors (@oiledits). There is an assumption that government officials are not neutral enough to edit Wikipedia articles.[17]

Wikipedians can be intolerant of unregistered users, so much so that a behavioral guideline was created on English Wikipedia called "Please do not bite the newcomers" as early as 2003.[18] Despite this measure, researchers discovered in 2013 that hostility toward newcomers was leading to a decline in active editors as good-faith contributions by newcomers were being harshly rejected.[19]

Different language Wikipedias tend to develop particular editing norms and display their own biases. The Egyptian Liberal was editing mostly English Wikipedia when those historic events took place in the Middle East in late 2010 and early 2011. When I asked him why he didn't edit Arabic Wikipedia or Egyptian Arabic Wikipedia, he told me that he started editing there but became frustrated and left to edit English Wikipedia instead.

"The Arabic was controlled by certain groups, and if you actually go land there and become an editor . . . and you actually cry to help improve the pages: it's just horrible. Because most people have a bias towards one side or another so the big two main groups on Wikipedia Arabic were either Islamist or pro government agents. . . . The numbers that try to write from a neutral point of view were very small."[20]

He said that on Arabic Wikipedia, debates were decided by voting and that editors voted in support of their friends and allies "no matter what," rather than debating "the quality of sources." He believed that some of the editors were working for the government, but others were just driven by political and religious beliefs.

The Egyptian Liberal recalled the article about the Liberal Islamic Movement that made him leave Arabic Wikipedia:

Other editors started adding Quaranic verses and sayings of the Prophet as a way to argue against the facts that I was including. . . . One guy was debating with me about one of the logos that we were using from Wikipedia Commons about Islamic Feminism, and he's like: "I need a source for it." I'm like: "Dude, we're using it from Wikipedia Commons. That's, like, the only one source for the actual picture." So . . . I left it at that and then some people just took out paragraphs from the article. But the arguments . . . they were really frustrating. I decided it would be best if instead of going in a vicious circle with them that I just leave it and they can do whatever they want, or delete it, and I'll edit Wikipedia in English.[21]

WIKIPEDIA: JANUARY 24, 2011

According to policy, Wikipedia should *follow* rather than *lead* when it comes to its coverage of current events. "Wikipedia is not a crystal ball," declares the pivotal content policy titled "What Wikipedia is not."[22] The encyclopedia "does not predict the future." Instead of leading the news by providing "first-hand news reports on breaking stories," Wikipedia should follow quietly behind, providing verifiable summaries of "reliable sources."

While the foreign press seems certain that protests will not erupt in Egypt, activist editors are determined that they will. Amid the relative silence of the foreign press, The Egyptian Liberal is hard at work, preparing the field for the arrival of a new article about the protests that he is hoping will be widespread.

In the weeks before the revolution in Egypt, the Egyptian Liberal had been helping to document protests in Tunisia and Algeria on English Wikipedia. The day before National Police Day, The Egyptian Liberal begins to prepare a Wikipedia article about the coming events. He doesn't publish the article immediately, instead uploading a series of images relating to the growing disquiet in Egypt to Wikimedia Commons, the sister site to Wikipedia, which houses images and video.

Wikimedia Commons is one of Wikimedia's fifteen projects, which include dictionaries, travel guides, textbooks, and an online newspaper. In addition to content projects that structure themselves around a particular media format (such as the encyclopedia), there are also sites whose primary purpose is to provide editors with space, infrastructure, and coordination tools. Meta-Wiki, for example, is a site where Wikipedians discuss requests for new language versions of Wikipedia, bid for Wikimedia Foundation grants, or vote on the election of stewards (Wikipedians with the highest levels of technical permissions across all Wikimedia projects).

The images that The Egyptian Liberal uploads to Wikimedia Commons are all political cartoons created by Brazilian cartoonist Carlos Latuff. The cartoon in figure 2.1 depicts a young man as a giant, wearing a gray hoodie emblazoned with "#JAN25." He is looking distastefully at a much smaller man in a pinstripe suit, whom he is holding between his finger and thumb. The cartoon's caption reads, "Khaled Mohamed Saeed holding up a tiny, flailing, stone-faced Hosni Mubarak."

The cartoon reflects a future that no one would have dreamed possible months earlier. Indeed, as I indicated earlier, the traditional press was relatively silent about Egypt's planned protests, and there were a few articles from prominent Western media outlets that explained why Egypt would not erupt like Tunisia had. Wikipedia claims to be an encyclopedia that follows the news rather than leads. But this cartoon (uploaded

2.1 "Khaled Mohamed Saeed holding up a tiny, flailing, stone-faced Hosni Mubarak," by Carlos Latuff.

to Wikimedia Commons and about to be used in the first version of the article) is explicitly a vision of the future—a future in which Egypt's victims rise up to defeat their perpetrators. Looming large in the image is the figure of the martyr that proved critical to widespread public support for the protests from all classes of Egyptian society. The image represents a dream about the future in which the martyr's death is avenged and the people revolt against their oppressors.

It seems strange for an encyclopedia to document history as it happens. But today, Wikipedia's editors readily create articles about current events. As I'm writing this, English Wikipedia's "In the news" headlines list both articles created as a result of events and existing articles that have been updated because of recent events. Dedicated articles relating to events have been created about the Australian bushfire season and the COVID-19 crisis, and existing articles have been updated to reflect current events (such as the UK officially leaving the European Union (EU) on January 31, 2020).

Articles about breaking news topics are peculiar to Wikipedia (traditional print encyclopedias only included events from the distant past), and although they are now the most popular articles on the site to edit and read, they weren't always recognized as a legitimate avenue for Wikipedia's encyclopedia work. Wikipedia's policy on the coverage of breaking news topics has evolved significantly since its founding in 2001.

This policy has fundamentally changed the way we think about the encyclopedic form. There is nothing natural or obvious about the ways in which Wikipedia's coverage of topics has evolved. The inclusion of current events developed out of the makeup of its dominant editor base and its origins at a pivotal moment in world history.

WIKIPEDIA AND THE RISE OF EVENTS

Wikipedia was founded in 2001 in the United States, eight months before two planes hit the Twin Towers in New York and the world was forever changed. Wikipedia scholar Brian Keegan[23] has eloquently described how Wikipedia's coverage of "breaking news" was a result of the debates about the profusion of articles that were catalyzed by those infamous attacks on September 11. In order to try to make sense of what had happened and to respond to the need for information about events as they unfolded, editors created almost a hundred articles around that time. In addition to information about the flights and buildings, about the military and economic responses to the events, there were also lists of casualties and survivors, personal recollections, and details about how to assist the relief effort, such as donating blood and money.

The debate about what to include on Wikipedia, however, focused on the creation of biographies for the victims and survivors of the attacks. Should Wikipedia include individuals simply because of their involvement in events? Or did more stringent criteria for inclusion need to be developed? After months of intense discussions, a consensus emerged among editors to move content related to victim memorials, tributes, personal experience, and general discussion to the September 11 Memorial Wiki[24] instead of incorporating it into the encyclopedia. According to Keegan, in so doing, Wikipedians banished content from the commemorative tradition while retaining elements from the journalistic tradition.

Keegan points out that this was the moment in which "newswork" was institutionalized on Wikipedia. It was during this period that a dedicated section for current events was created, and it was where debates about which articles were sufficiently important or still timely enough to merit inclusion ensued. It was also during this time that a series of policies were developed to clarify the boundaries of newswork on the encyclopedia.

The "Wikipedia is not" policy was first developed in August 2002, and the editor, Stephen Gilbert, introduced news to the policy during its initial edits. He wrote, "Wikipedia should not offer news reports on breaking stories,"[25] but added, "creating background 'encyclopedia' articles on topics currently in the news is an excellent idea." But what does that mean, exactly? When Britons went to the polls to vote in the EU referendum of 2016, for example, an article about the EU could be useful. If an earthquake struck Haiti, articles about Haiti and earthquakes might find grateful readers. When Nelson Mandela died, his Wikipedia biography would be helpful reading. What is not appropriate, according to this first instantiation of the rule, is the creation of news articles about the events *themselves*.

In the next edits, however, Wikipedians added another sentence to the policy to reflect the affordances of the wiki to articles dedicated to events: "But of course, the Wiki process lends itself to collaborative, up-to-the-minute construction of current and ongoing events of historical significance."[26] As long as the event was significant, in other words, then Wikipedians should make the most of the wiki's affordances to develop articles that documented events.

The policy has since evolved to clarify what constitutes acceptable newsworthy topics for inclusion, as well as the appropriate style and content for articles of this type. Articles need to contain verifiable information (rather than be firsthand accounts), be about "historically significant" topics and events, and be written in encyclopedic format rather than "news style." A policy on "notability," particularly for events, was also developed. Often referred to as Wikipedia:EVENT, it was promoted to full guideline status in December 2009 and has a five-pronged test to establish the notability of events.

A defining characteristic of experienced Wikipedians is in their identification as either "inclusionists" or "exclusionists." For inclusionists, "Wikipedia is not paper,"[27] which means that editors should be encouraged to include as much information about the world as possible. These editors take a broader view of encyclopedic notability guidelines when deciding whether a topic warrants a Wikipedia article. Exclusionists, however, believe that Wikipedia needs to play a stricter gatekeeping role by limiting what is included in the encyclopedia to only "notable" topics. Notability on Wikipedia is generally defined as topics that have gained significant attention "by the world at large and over a period of time." [28] Wikipedians rely on evidence of notability from external sources in the media, academic and scientific publishing, and other "reliable sources."

In the context of current events, the policy[29] stipulates that an event should have lasting effects and wide geographical impact. Another requirement relates to the depth, duration, and diversity of coverage by journalists. The policy forbids the creation of articles relating to "routine coverage" of wedding announcements, obituaries, sports scores, criminal acts, or people notable for only a single event. It warns against rushing to create articles, but also against rushing to delete them. "Early coverage of events may lack perspective and be subject to factual errors." The policy asserts, however, that "articles about widely reported major unexpected or unprecedented events such as the 2004 Indian Ocean earthquake, the Assassination of Benazir Bhutto or the Death of Michael Jackson will almost certainly gain consensus to be kept even when created on the same day as the event occurred."

Wikipedia policy about what constitutes a notable event assumes agreement on what constitutes a "major" or "unprecedented" event. It assumes that everyone would naturally recognize the importance of the death of Michael Jackson, for example, even in its earliest stages. But every designation of the notable event status requires a prediction about its import, and that prediction is subjective—that is, it is a position from somewhere, from a particular location and perspective, coming out of a particular view of the world. How would Wikipedia's predominantly white, North American and European editors interpret the Wikipedia:EVENT policy regarding a foreign invasion in Kenya versus one in the United States, for example? I learned the answer to this question in 2011 when I first started studying Wikipedia in earnest.

A QUESTION OF SIGNIFICANCE

In 2011, I was working for a Kenyan nonprofit technology company called Ushahidi. We were trying to figure out how to build tools to help people who collaboratively curate stories during high-volume news events—especially when they are physically distant from one another—and were looking to Wikipedia to understand how Wikipedia editors did this work so successfully.

In late 2011, I arrived in Nairobi for a visit to Ushahidi's headquarters. After checking in at a local guest house, I went straight to the local supermarket and bought copies of every local newspaper. It was a big news day in the country because of reports that the Kenyan Army had invaded southern Somalia to root out the militant group Al-Shabaab. The newspapers sported bold headlines announcing the invasion, and images showed Kenyan military tanks and other scenes from the offensive.

On the ground in Nairobi, it was difficult to avoid the pervasiveness of the event. Everyone was talking about it: on television and in newspapers, in supermarkets and bars, on local Twitter and Facebook feeds. For Kenyans, this story had significance; it had meaning beyond the simple fact of the Kenyan military moving into Somalia. It was a story about security and independence; it was about the Kenyan military trying to prove itself. It was the first time since independence that the army had been involved in an active campaign, and the public was watching to see whether it would succeed. This was also a story about revenge. Foreign aid workers and tourists had been kidnapped on the Kenyan side of the border with southern Somalia—one of Kenya's major tourist destinations—and the British government advised Britons against traveling there, which was a blow to the many Kenyans who relied heavily on tourist income. The country had endured painful attacks by Al-Shabaab, and the public believed that something needed to be done.

In response to the Kenyan offensive, there were threats of retaliation by Al-Shabaab, many sympathizers of whom were living inside Kenya. One night during this time, I was sitting in a bar with friends and remarked how quiet it was. My friends answered that everyone had been urged not to go out—and especially not to bars—because of the threat of reprisals. That same night, Al-Shabaab acted on those threats at a bar in the city center only a few miles away from us. Two years later, Al-Shabaab directed a mass shooting at the Westgate shopping mall, killing seventy-one and wounding two hundred.

I noticed after a quick search on Wikipedia that a page had been created to document the event but that it had already been nominated for deletion by one of English Wikipedia's editors on the grounds that it did not meet Wikipedia's notability criteria. The nominator, Middayexpress, wrote that the event was a minor "incursion" rather than an "invasion" and that it was "routine" for troops from neighboring countries to cross the border for military operations.[30] Middayexpress wrote that another recent invasion of Somalia, the UN-sanctioned Ethiopian intervention, had no separate article devoted to it and was merely covered in the body of the "War on Somalia (2006–2009)" article. According to Middayexpress, the policy was that "notable events usually receive coverage beyond a relatively short news cycle,"[31] and this event was being covered by only a few news sites and without extensive analysis.

A week later, a decision was made to keep the article after multiple editors chimed in to argue for its significance. One user, Collinsakala, voted to keep the article and responded to the deletion proposal with the following: "Wikipedia is not for Americans only. This event is very (noteworthy) for the African reader of (W)ikipedia."[32]

Kenyans understood very well the significance of their army moving into Somalia to attack Al-Shabaab. It touched their lives deeply, affected their daily choices, and contributed to a heightened sense of anxiety and fear. To see Wikipedians arguing that this was not notable enough for inclusion in the encyclopedia was offensive to Kenyans. They recognized all too well the attitudes of editors outside Africa making judgments about what was important to their country.

To me, this experience demonstrated that, even in relation to Wikipedia, all knowledge is *situated*, as the feminist scholar of science and technology Donna Haraway argued in her famous piece "Situated Knowledges."[33] Knowledge about what was important and therefore what should be included in Wikipedia was contextual. The determination of what actually *constituted* knowledge (versus mere conjecture) was situated. Like all knowledge, it came *from* somewhere. Many Wikipedians denied this when they framed their own situated understanding about the event in the form of facts ("this is a mere incursion," "it is a routine event"), as though they could somehow see, from above, the situation for what it truly was. They did this without any trace of themselves in the statements, refusing to admit that theirs were views *from* somewhere.

In his excellent book about Wikipedia, *Wikipedia and the Politics of Openness*, Nathaniel Tkacz[34] writes that Wikipedia's refusal to admit the work it does in framing the world does damage to those whose knowledge it excludes. Examining the "frame wars" relating to the images of Muhammed on English Wikipedia, Tkacz writes about the damage that is done through disputes like the one that ensued when images of Muhammed were included in the article about the prophet. "The wrong is threefold: the object of concern (the Muhammed entry) appears in a way that is considered deeply offensive; the discussion statements are deemed illegitimate; and those who express them are in turn marked as biased, religious fundamentalists, deceitful, angry and so on."[35]

Wikipedia tries to distance itself from truth battles outside the encyclopedia by adopting a view that truth can be discovered outside Wikipedia in "reliable sources." But Wikipedia has developed a whole set of rules that help editors establish the truth of a particular statement—"a truth defined or restricted," writes Tkacz, "by what is neutral, non-original, published, reliable, attributable and verifiable." Tkacz writes that this isn't because Wikipedia is evil or wrong, but just that it "exists because of and not in distinction of the truth." Rather than dismissing Wikipedia for "abandoning the truth," Tkacz urges us to rather attend to the "procedures in which the truth of Wikipedia is established."[36]

Wikipedia's claim to neutrality in the context of current events is that it does not make decisions about what constitutes a historic event because it defers to what "reliable sources" are indicating as significant. And yet, editors are clearly making important, situated decisions about (a) what *constitutes* a "reliable source" and (b) what constitutes *importance* according to those sources. This is why the location of editors matters so much to the knowledge that is ultimately produced. It means that if Kenyans dominated English Wikipedia's editor community, there would clearly have been no debate about the importance of this event, even at its earliest stages. In order for facts to travel well on Wikipedia, especially when they are about subjects located outside of Wikipedia editors' purview, they need to carry with them a *story* that will travel well. They need allies who have mastered Wikipedia's frame and who are able to speak from Wikipedia's vantage point which appears to rise above the messiness of knowledge politics that dominate the sources below.

A SPACE OF MULTIPLE POSSIBILITIES

In Egypt, our story begins in the space of possibility before the January 25 protests actually took place. It is a space of planning, of voices, of speeches, of impassioned dialogue. In the weeks before they congregated in Tahrir Square on January 25, people met in the social media spaces that had recently been opened up to them.

On Wikipedia, this was the moment before the first version of the article that would become "Egyptian Revolution of 2011" was created. It was the period before the event came to public attention and remained on the margins of political consciousness. Change was afoot, talked about on the ground and particularly on the internet in Egypt, but outside the country there was little widespread awareness of the disquiet.

The moment before a new article is created on Wikipedia is one of enormous possibility. Wikipedia presents itself as a site that "anyone can edit," and it may seem that articles can include "any thing." Possibilities for writing of history as it happens, then, may seem endless. But Wikipedia is a frame in which only certain knowledges can fit.

When The Egyptian Liberal publishes the Carlos Latuff cartoons to Wikimedia Commons and starts preparing his article about the coming protests, he does so with an understanding of Wikipedia's frame. Like other social media platforms, such as Twitter and Facebook, Wikipedia is an ideal avenue for the voices of Egyptian activists at this early stage. Unlike the local traditional press, which is largely controlled by government, or the international press, which is either unaware or disinterested, Wikipedia is relatively open to Egyptian activists, and articles on English Wikipedia are widely read by an international audience, particularly from the United States. Wikipedians have significant agency in determining what is covered on the encyclopedia. They independently determine what is covered by responding to the attention the event is receiving around them. Wikipedia is a viable space for activists to cocreate historic events.

The problem is that, unlike Facebook and Twitter, Wikipedia has multiple rules and processes that restrict what can be written there: rules for writing about current events, automated processes that influence what can be accounted for, and dynamics particular to the platform that need to be taken into account when deciding what knowledge can be included about the events to come. Wikipedians are reluctant to write about current events too soon, before their importance is known, and before reliable sources have given their own accounts. In order to provide sources in the article, The Egyptian Liberal will rely on people turning out to protest and the journalists who will cover those protests. He will rely on his mastery of the frame in order to ensure that Wikipedia policy is interpreted in favor of the protests.

The Egyptian pro-democracy April 6 Youth Movement chooses January 25—National Police Day—for the protests. Local celebrities, local football fans, and opposition parties join tens of thousands of people in announcing on the Facebook page for the event that they will be attending the demonstrations. Coordinators of the protest declare their demands in the run-up to the protests: the emergency law that has been in place for decades and used to suspend constitutional rights and curb nongovernmental political activity needs to be lifted, and minimum wages need to be increased. On January 25 itself, now dubbed "the Day of Rage," protests are due to kick off at two o'clock in Cairo and across the country.

In preparing the article about the upcoming protests, The Egyptian Liberal has been more prescient than perhaps he realizes: Egypt is about to erupt.

3

ERUPTION

In the winter of 2017, I was re-analyzing the first traces of the 2011 Egyptian revolution article, using the history tab of English Wikipedia's interface. The history page of an article is like a huge vault, hosting summarized records of every edit made to the article since its creation.

There had been over eight thousand edits at the time, but I clicked on the "oldest" and scrolled down the page. And there it was:

> 13:26, 25 January 2011 The Egyptian Liberal (talk|contribs) . . (2,336 bytes) (+2,336) . . (←Created page with '{{New unreviewed article|source=ArticleWizard|date={{subst:CURRENTMONTHNAME}} {{subst:CURRENTYEAR}}}} {{Expert-subject|Politics|date=January 2011}} {{current relate . . .')(thank)[1]

To a nonexpert, the summary reads like a hieroglyph—a foreign text punctuated by curly brackets, arrows and vertical bars (|), referrals to "bytes," and unfamiliar abbreviations. It is data that is the result of automation and thus appears perfect. To a Wikipedian, though, the summary is bursting with information about the context of the article and its creation, as well as what is missing or broken in the record. This single trace marks the moment of creation.

The summary tells the time of the first draft, who wrote it, the size of the edit, what the status of the article was at the time, and how it was created. To an experienced eye, the trace also shows sign of decay and malfunctioning. The code and templates that drive these automated functions are constantly being updated and refined, and so understanding an old record requires knowledge of how Wikipedia evolves through changing practice, rules, and standards.

The trace of the edit as summarized in the history page provides for a series of editing functions. By clicking on either the editor's "talk" page or the term "thank," users may contact the editor or thank them for their edit (a gesture similar to a Facebook "like"). Other hyperlinked terms allow for the rapid examination (and evaluation) of an editor's contributions through a special viewing pane, also in summarized form. Much of the collaborative editing practice is about trying to work out the intent of editors, particularly when they make significant edits like this to start a new article. Being able to rapidly evaluate an editor and their past behavior becomes essential to the daily work of keeping Wikipedia free from harmful content.

This trace contains two clues about the context of the article's creation. These clues are warning flags to editors: they flag practices by inexperienced users, whom Wikipedians are generally very wary of. The first warning flag is that the article was clearly created using Wikipedia's Article Wizard, originally built to allow unregistered users to create articles that would then be reviewed by more experienced editors. The Article Wizard triggers procedures involving much more scrutiny (and potentially a longer wait) than if the author had created the article without it. The process of creation and review, known as Articles for Creation, is part of a peer review process where any registered editor can either accept a submitted article or decline it because it appears to be unsuitable for Wikipedia.

The second potential warning flag is that the article is identified as being related to current events (referred to by the "current related" tag). This means that the article is subject to rules that forbid Wikipedians from representing events too soon after they have occurred. This, too, could have resulted in the article being put up for deletion.

I wanted to go through the creation process as The Egyptian Liberal would have done. I could see that he used the Article Wizard to create the article, so I too used the tool in the process of writing a new article.

Although registered editors can use the Wizard, the tool is designed for the new, inexperienced user. It simplifies (and standardizes) the process of article creation on Wikipedia by guiding editors through a series of steps and rules required to start a new article. Going through the step-by-step process, I realize that the Wizard is as much about warning new editors about creating new articles as it is about helping them. Some important elements must be found before an article can exist, the software reminds us. These include "reliable sources" and a "notable," "encyclopedic" subject. If these elements are not present, the software sends editors to other parts of the encyclopedia and sister projects, ostensibly to pursue other tasks.

The Wizard asks whether the article I want to create is about "a recent event." When I choose "yes," I am taken to a page that encourages me to write an article on Wikinews rather than on Wikipedia. The process stops here. Wikinews is a separate Wikimedia project, one in which authors are able to create single-authored articles written in news style about journalistic topics. It is much less popular than Wikipedia, and the site produces very few daily articles.

The software, in other words, is explicitly prohibiting me from starting a new article if it is about a breaking news event.[2] In order to evade this process, I needed to avoid choosing the "recent event" option and instead choose the "something else" option from the dropdown topics menu. This is what The Egyptian Liberal must have done. This strategic action is just one of many that divide experienced Wikipedians from first-time editors. Editors must know how the coded processes work on Wikipedia in order to know how to (sometimes) evade them.

MAKING A SPACE

In order to facilitate the representation of events in Wikipedia, a space needs to be created for the future recording of facts surrounding the event. The ideal form of space creation in Wikipedia is the creation of an article. The new article contains no baggage of previous articles, with their embedded authors, narrative frames, and teeming desires. But in order to ensure that the article about to be published endures, its author would have to prove the historical significance of the event. Only notable events warrant inclusion in Wikipedia's archive, and notability of events this early requires careful maneuvering.

This is a difficult task at such an early stage, and so it proves for The Egyptian Liberal. Few traditional media sources have yet reported on events and their significance (remember that they largely haven't seen this coming, and Western media don't have their own correspondents on the ground yet). He does what he can by drawing in companions—in the form of available sources and links to other Wikipedia articles and categories—and by reaching out for the support of allies (other editors) who might do the important bureaucratic work of approving the article and thus facilitating its inclusion in the archive.

The authors of sources outside of Wikipedia who are cited in the article are shipped in to support its statements and constitute an important ally. They speak on behalf of the facts; their knowledge and authority become important for the stability and validity of the article as a whole. Editors are allies who work with others to firmly root the article into the fabric of Wikimedia and across the wider web. They are critical for fortifying the article against uncertainty and attack.

On Wikipedia, volunteer labor is a scarce resource; the most important allies are a critical mass of other editors and their bots, who can help support the growth of the article. It would be impossible for Wikipedia to maintain its repository of almost fifty-four million articles without the aid of bots. Bots are automated tools, configured by Wikipedians, that perform repetitive and mundane tasks on the encyclopedia, including checking new edits for potential vandalism, correcting grammar errors, and reformatting citations. But bots also enforce rules concerning how editors relate to one another. Stuart Geiger, who has written extensively about the significance of the work that bots do on Wikipedia, gives the example of the Wikipedia policy called the Three Revert Rule or 3RR. This rule prohibits an editor reversing another's edits more than three times in a twenty-four-hour period on a particular article. A bot named 3RRBot scans for such violations and reports them to administrators.[3]

FIRST TRACE

It is the morning of January 25, 2011. The Egyptian Liberal has attended political protests in Egypt in the past, and he told me in an interview that the police usually outnumbered the protesters. When he joined a protest about the minimum wage the previous year, for example, there were only a handful of protesters. Today, The Egyptian Liberal joins one of the Cairo protests with some of his friends from high school. Expecting the same handful of people as before, they are shocked to discover thousands of people in the streets. Large numbers of protesters are gathering in cities across Egypt. In Cairo, protesters break through the security cordon outside the High Court in the center of the city. They move to Tahrir Square (Liberation Square), where police fire tear gas, water cannons, and rubber bullets to drive them from the square. Protesters, in turn, hurl rocks at police and chant "Down with Mubarak."

At 3:26 p.m. local time (1:26 p.m. UTC), The Egyptian Liberal publishes the first version of an article on English Wikipedia. It is titled "2011 Egyptian Protests" and consists of four sentences, a single source, a list of related Wikipedia articles, six categories, and an infobox with a cartoon image and the date of the event.

At the moment of the article's creation, The Egyptian Liberal produces a new space in which events might be recorded as they happened on Wikipedia. The endurance of this space, like a front line in enemy territory, is not inevitable. It is not a fait accompli that the article will be allowed to continue. Its position needs to be defended.

In publishing the article and continuing to add stabilizing elements, The Egyptian Liberal performs the essential work of articulating the significance of the event, just as multiple other actors are doing in media organizations and across social media platforms around the world at this time. This is an important act of creation in which events are framed in ways that will endure long after thousands of edits have been made. The article at this moment does not merely reflect the world as it is in some unattached manner. In the creation of the article and its acceptance into the archive, The Egyptian Liberal frames the narrative of events in fundamental ways. That framing is performed not necessarily to convince *readers* of the subject matter's importance but to convince its *editors*.

Wikipedia's editors are patrolling new articles with the assistance of automated tools that mark up the articles according to some of the traces of their construction. Those traces include evidence of the authoring editor's edit experience, the existence of categories in the article, and links to other Wikipedia articles. If the article does not contain categories and links, it will be flagged as potentially harmful. If its author is a new editor, it will be similarly negatively perceived.

With some experience of the ways in which Wikipedia works, The Egyptian Liberal creates a first version of the article containing the important elements of categories and internal links to other Wikipedia articles. Facts are clustered within coded objects in the article: a title, a lead paragraph, an infobox, a reference, and a series of categories and hyperlinks to other Wikipedia articles. Each of these objects is encoded with data that notifies Wikipedians about the possible harmful nature of the article and enables differential velocity or potential for travel.

The ways in which objects are coded results in some objects (and their constituent facts) being heavier than others, more or less stable to change and mutation. But facts are not only composed of data. They are embedded with symbolism that establishes the "we" of the protests and positions key stakeholders in the event as either victims or perpetrators. The first version of the article lasts only eleven minutes before it is edited. But this first version contains vital information about how the event narrative was originally constructed, using particular types of evidence, referring to certain symbols and identities, and applying "grammars" of construction available to Wikipedians.

The first elements of the article that need to be inserted are the title and introductory material, and they are critical for ensuring the article's endurance. They will also serve to classify the new article. Classification is the work of genre creation on the encyclopedia, and it will determine what type of narrative follows. The event genre, in opposition to biographical articles, or articles about natural or technological phenomena, must include facts that reflect what happened, to whom it happened, and why it happened. Importantly, significant events circle around the question of responsibility: the determination of the legitimate victims, perpetrators, and authorities on the event. Who are the actors in this tragedy? Who are its witnesses? Why is this a significant break from the past?

Let's examine each of the elements in the first version of the article, paying attention to the standards for their material and symbolic composition.

TITLE

The first version of the article is titled "2011 Egyptian Protests." The title establishes the ontological category of the article (in this case, an event) and the location of the event in time and space (2011, Egypt). As Robin Wagner-Pacifici writes, "The first representation is the label of an event as a particular kind."[4] The title of the article sets up a range of possibilities for how the events could be described, but there is little room for the article space to transform into an article about a person or place. The title also establishes the first fact under our microscope: that events are taking place in Egypt in the year 2011 and that these events are most accurately described as "protests." Another statement that lies beneath the explicit ones is that the events happening today (January 25, 2011) are significant enough to be singled out from all the other protest events that have happened in Egypt.

How is the title encoded? And how does this enable possibilities for travel? Titles on Wikipedia identify the unique records of items in the database of a single language version. Coded article titles mean that these objects are not static. Articles can have alternate names, and sometimes article titles are changed as events evolve or as naming conventions change. There can be only one "2011 Egyptian Protests" article on English Wikipedia, but there can be multiple alternative titles.

Alternative titles are linked to the canonical article using redirects—code that directs users to the canonical version even when they have entered a different search term. At the time of writing there were fifty-nine redirects (or alternative names) for the article. If you type "2011 Egyptian riots," "Youth Revolution," or "Jade Revolution" into Wikipedia's search box, you will be automatically redirected to the title "Egyptian Revolution of 2011," which editors have decided is the most appropriate, according to Wikipedia's current naming conventions.

Article titles also serve as links between different Wikipedia language editions. The "Egyptian Revolution of 2011" article is currently linked to fifty-nine other language versions and one version in Simple Wikipedia, which is written in "basic English." I say "versions," but Polish Wikipedia, for example, may share only the title of an article and bear little similarity to the content of the English Wikipedia article.

Wikipedia editors have developed conventions (codified in rules and according to practice) for titles in order to provide a unique key for locating the article in the database and to establish consistency across the project. According to Wikipedia naming conventions, article titles are "short, natural, distinguishable and recognizable."[5] Titles serve the goal of discoverability, an essential feature of the way in which Wikipedia functions as a reference source.

Titles for articles relating to events[6] should indicate when the event happened, where it happened, and what happened. Ideally, they should indicate the "common name" for the event, where "common name" is the name that "most English speakers who are aware of the topic" use. Conflicts often arise when editors disagree about what is the quintessential title that alternative titles will redirect to, and when there is an attempt to provide an association that some editors believe is inaccurate or misleading. An example of an event title in the style guide is the article titled "War in Darfur." Authors of the guide write that, although the term "Darfur genocide" is also used, "there is no general scholarly agreement on this yet."

LEAD AND BODY TEXT

Similar in shape and form to a dictionary definition, the first sentences of a Wikipedia article serve as a summary of the phenomenon's important features. The lead is constructed as factual statements in the form of an extended dictionary definition that answers key questions about the phenomenon—its ontological status. Is this "thing" an event, a person, a place, an object? What are its important features? Why is it significant? What are the key controversies surrounding it?

In this case, the lead text of the first version of the article contains four sentences defining and categorizing the events in Egypt and explaining why the protests are notable. Notice the mixed use of tenses. Editors can get confused when writing about events that are still happening . . . especially if English is not their native language.

> [sentence 1] The 2011 Egyptian protests are a continuing series of street demonstrations taking place throughout Egypt from January 2010 onwards with organizers counting on the Tunisian uprising to inspire the crowds to mobilize.
>
> [sentence 2] The demonstrations and riots were reported to have started over police brutality, State of Emergency Laws, unemployment, the lack of housing, food inflation, corruption, freedom of speech and poor living conditions.
>
> [sentence 3] The protests main goal is to oust President Hosni Mubarak who has been in power for more than 30 years.

[sentence 4] While localized protests were already commonplace over previous years, major protests and riots erupted all over the country starting in "25 January" (*the date set by Egyptian opposition groups, celebrities, and football supporters for a major demonstration*).

A number of important facts are stated within this first version of the article. The ontological status of the phenomenon is established by the structure of the first sentence: "The 2011 Egyptian protests are . . ." But the main work that the lead is doing is establishing notability. The events are linked to an already notable subject in Wikipedia's database, the "Tunisian uprising" article. The next sentence embeds the article further into Wikipedia's database with links to seven other Wikipedia articles about general sociological and political concepts such as "unemployment," "corruption," and "freedom of speech."

The lead text of an article is a relatively flexible element and is often changed to reflect the article's subject more accurately as the phenomenon evolves—especially in the case of breaking news events in which information is iteratively released as more becomes known. The lead is an important feature of the article because it is often the only text that is read. It is also important because it is often extracted by other sites (such as search engines and digital assistants) that make use of Wikipedia for descriptions of phenomena.

INFOBOX

The third element that The Egyptian Liberal adds to the article is the infobox. Infoboxes are a popular form of information representation that are found in a wide variety of publications. In news stories, they are often highlighted in the text to itemize the key facts about a subject as well as links to related stories. Almost all of the six million articles on English Wikipedia feature an infobox, representing a range of different categories—from facts about a politician's nationality to the birth and death dates of Jim Kirk, a fictional character from the *Star Trek* series.[7]

According to Wikipedia documentation, infoboxes serve two key audiences.[8] The first audience is the readers of Wikipedia. Infoboxes serve this group by providing a summary of unifying aspects that the articles share and by improving navigation to other interrelated articles. All infoboxes relating to people, for example, include a person's date of birth. Accessing the infobox for Jim Kirk, one should easily be able to navigate to the actor who first portrayed him, William Shatner.

But infoboxes also serve a second audience: computers. The same documentation on Wikipedia's infoboxes notes that "many infoboxes also emit structured metadata" and that this metadata is used by "third party re-users."[9] The machinery behind the infobox, in other words, includes metadata (or data about data) that explains to other computers connected to Wikipedia's live database what type of thing that information represents and how that subject is connected to other entities. Jim Kirk, for example, represents a person who is also male and a fictional character who is played by an actor named William Shatner. Infoboxes are alive—in the sense that they are connected to other infoboxes on entirely independent websites via the algorithms that feed them.

Infoboxes are highly structured data elements. The fact that multiple pages or articles use the same vocabulary to define the characteristics of an event means that infoboxes are probably the most important location for facts in an article because they can be rapidly spread to sites far beyond the article space. Infoboxes contain rocket fuel for facts, providing the force and shape necessary for them to travel to other sites.

Events infobox categories are not necessarily mutually exclusive. There is an infobox for "events," in addition to "civil conflicts" and "civilian attacks." Some infoboxes are used much more heavily than others: the "civilian attack" infobox, for example, is used in almost 2,000 articles, while the "civil conflict" event is used in fewer than 450 articles. The "robbery incident" infobox is used in only three articles.

The key differences between infoboxes are in the fields used to populate them. In this case, the (now discontinued) "uprising" infobox had fields for location, date, and characteristics. The Egyptian Liberal populates the uprising infobox by attributing a value to six of the parameters, leaving other parameters (including "injuries" and "fatalities") blank. He specifies the title of the infobox ("2011 Egyptian protests"), the file name of the image ("Khaled Mohamed Saeed holding up a tiny, flailing, stone-faced Hosni Mubarak.png"), the caption for the image ("Khaled Mohamed Saeed holding up a tiny, flailing, stone-faced Hosni Mubarak"), the location of the event using the Egyptian flag icon, the dates of the event ("25 January 2011—*ongoing*"), and its characteristics ("demonstrations, riots, self-immolation").[10]

The cartoon image of Khaled Mohamed Saeed and Hosni Mubarak is an unusual addition to the infobox. Usually, infoboxes about events include a single photograph depicting some unifying aspect of the event, but this is a reminder of how early in the event the article has been published. The Egyptian Liberal told me that he had actually prepared the article the day before the protests were scheduled. Obviously no images were available at this stage for The Egyptian Liberal to use. He uses the cartoon, even though it is not ideal, because images are necessary to make the article appear as legitimate as possible.

SOURCES AND CITATIONS

One of the most important objects in the article frame is the source and its citation. Sources are necessary companions for the travel of facts on Wikipedia, and the practice of citation is fundamental to Wikipedia epistemology. Editors use citations during breaking news events to back up claims being made, and as a trail for users to follow in order to verify whether the sources are being accurately reflected. The discovery, triangulation, selection, and summarizing of sources are central to the practice of article editing, and sourcing practice plays an important role in determining the framing of events.

As we saw in the previous chapter, all three of Wikipedia's core content policies—NPOV, no original research, and verifiability—are centered on how Wikipedians should use sources and which sources are deemed to be "reliable."

The Egyptian Liberal cites a single Agence France-Presse (AFP) article both at the end of the sentence giving the reasons for the protests and in the final sentence explaining why the January 25 protests are notable. AFP is a useful companion for the facts in the article, especially at this early stage, because it is a widely recognized English-language source that is easily accessible (with no paywalls or reading restrictions).

The choice of sources to back up factual claims made in the article is critically important to the travel of facts. Bad citation companions can stop an article dead in its tracks; good ones can provide the fuel necessary for the further travel of facts. A source that editors working on the article deem to be unreliable could result in the removal of facts from the article; a source recognized as reliable and trustworthy usually results in the further rooting of the article into Wikipedia's infrastructure.

CATEGORIES

The first version of the article contains a series of links: first, to related articles and "portals," where work based on particular topics is coordinated; and, second, to categories of articles. Each link cluster serves to embed the article in Wikipedia's database, further stabilizing the article in order to stave off attacks. Connecting to portals also brings in other editors to help improve the article, since adding a new article triggers a notification to editors watching portal pages.

The process of categorization serves to connect events in Egypt to phenomena in a manner that actively constructs the narrative of the event. Categories in the "See also" section connect the events in Egypt to protests in Tunisia and Algeria that are much further along. Other categories classify the events as "riots" and "protest marches."

BUILDING DEFENSES

Over the next three hours, The Egyptian Liberal continues to work alone on the article. He shores up facts and shapes them according to Wikipedia's rules and standards, thereby establishing a defensive position for the tide that will inevitably break as news of the events in Egypt spreads. He makes both small changes (changing the access date of the news sources cited in the article) and large changes (adding paragraphs and rearranging material).

In doing so, The Egyptian Liberal sketches out narrative threads of the event by identifying its victims, perpetrators, and legitimate witnesses. The victims of the story are clearly at the center of the first editions of the article. In the second edit, The Egyptian Liberal introduces a background section to the article and creates a table with four "self-immolation" incidents that provides the names and details of the Egyptians who were reported to have set themselves on fire as protests, thus mimicking the suicide of Mohamed Bouazizi a few weeks prior. In addition to their names, the table has a field for "status." Only one person has died so far.

In one of the next edits, The Egyptian Liberal provides a citation for the statement indicating the goals of the protesters: "The protests main goal is to oust President Hosni Mubarak who has been in power for more than 30 years." The citation is to an AFP Berlin article published by *Daily News Egypt* that summarized an interview with Egyptian opposition leader Mohamed ElBaradei, published by the German news magazine *Der Spiegel* on January 25. The *Der Spiegel* article quotes ElBaradei as saying that Egyptians should be able to follow Tunisians' lead, but nowhere in the interview does he explicitly declare that the goal of the protesters is to oust Mubarak. The Egyptian Liberal has constructed a new factual claim where its companion is just for show: it does not truly verify the statement it accompanies.

The Egyptian Liberal continues to prepare the article for the addition of statements he predicts will be necessary. He creates an "arrests" section, which he leaves empty. The infobox reads "ongoing" in place of an end date. The "self-immolations" table is ready for martyrs to be added to it. He then starts to document the protester numbers as they are being reported.

In filling out the details of the event, The Egyptian Liberal also demonstrates who he believes are the legitimate witnesses of events in the context of Wikipedia practice. Although the Facebook group We Are All Khaled Said was an important feature of the protests, it is not cited until days later. Social media is illegitimate in the context of Wikipedia's rules and policies; the reliable sources policy explicitly warns against the inclusion of social media sources. Legitimate witnesses at this stage are largely drawn from the traditional press, with nine sources (all English language) included—mostly articles from Reuters, AFP, and CNN. The Media Line, which describes itself as an American nonprofit news agency "dedicated to reporting from the Middle East and Ya Libnan that is staffed by volunteers,"[11] is the only nonmainstream news source.

The Egyptian Liberal offers his own representation of events through the prism of Wikipedia policy and practice. He has selected facts and their companions in order to develop a defensive position against attack by those who might discredit the article. He has also offered a representation of the "we" of the protests to include all Egyptians and connected the protests to the recently successful Tunisian revolution through his unification of protesters' goals and his connection, via categories, to that event.

He has labeled the victims of the story as those who have set themselves alight in response to the desperate conditions in Egypt, as well as Khaled Mohamed Saeed, who was murdered by police. He has also labeled the perpetrator by actively constructing a single goal of ousting Mubarak, even though there is no clear mechanism by which protesters' demands are being collectively articulated at this early stage. By associating his statements of fact with companions from the traditional English-language media, while leaving out social media, The Egyptian Liberal also articulates who the legitimate witnesses of the event are.

As Wagner-Pacifici notes about the progress of historic events, "Uptake is critical to make labels stick."[12] For the article to establish the credibility necessary for its long-term endurance, other editors must accept the article into Wikipedia's collection, and The Egyptian Liberal's initial framing of the article is critical for this to occur.

RECRUITING EDITORS

When the article is created, it is automatically flagged as belonging to the category "Unreviewed new articles created via the Article Wizard from January 2011." The use of the Wizard means that the article needs to be reviewed by one other editor (that is, the editor simply removes the tag) in order to be accepted. In 2011, anyone other than the creator could remove the "new unreviewed article" tag. Alternatively, they might tag it for deletion or, if it needs additional work, for "cleanup."

Around the time The Egyptian Liberal created the article, the number of new articles being created using this process was about thirty per day. The editors reviewing articles had gone on a backlog drive so that new articles would be reviewed within a few days. The acceptance rate was only about 30 percent.

As soon as the article is published, a series of notifications ring out across the encyclopedia, calling out to members of different work groups to assess and help improve the article. The notification processes are automatically triggered by his use of the Wizard and by his inclusion of certain tags.

The Article Wizard software automatically adds the article to a growing list of new, unreviewed articles in what is called the New Pages Feed, ready for experienced editors to review them. The article is still public and available but contains a warning tag that it is a "new unreviewed article." Rejection could see the article immediately deleted if it is considered to be an attack page or a copyright violation, or if it is perceived that there is "no indication of importance." Alternatively, an editor could propose it for deletion using a more deliberative process.

Page curation involves the review of new pages on Wikipedia using software that makes rapid decision-making easier. An interface provides a list of all incoming new page submissions to Wikipedia in real time, and curation tools enable editors to quickly review, tag for maintenance, nominate for deletion, or leave help and advice tips for the page creator.[13]

One of the key features of the software and the practice of page review is the ability to rapidly remove what Wikipedia calls "bad-faith contributions," such as "attack pages" or copyright violations. The feed enables editors to view metadata related to the article, such as who "patrolled" (reviewed) the article or whether it has been nominated for deletion, as well as data about the article itself (its size, a preview of the text, whether it has been categorized, and how many users have contributed to it). Page patrollers' first view of an article is through its data.

For the best chance of survival, an article should contain the data elements that will avoid the triggering of warnings in the page review software. Each new article is summarized with data about the number of categories, references, the size of the article, and data about the author (notably, how many edits they have performed). Importantly, the categories and references need to be properly formatted using Wikitext if they are to be visible as data here. Without the right category tags, these groupings will not be accounted for.

Subject matter portals and pages like the New Pages Feed are two of the many gateways to Wikipedia's database that are used by editors to coordinate work across particular types of articles or themes of work. Portals act as entry points for collections of articles, images, and categories around particular topics. Like other classification mechanisms, portals assist editors in finding tasks related to particular subject areas on Wikipedia and provide readers and editors with a mechanism for navigating Wikipedia topics.

When The Egyptian Liberal constructs the first version of the article, he does so by including

{{Expert-subject|Politics|date=January 2011}}

This means that members of the WikiProject: Politics group are automatically alerted to the existence of the new article and invited to participate in its development. This link automatically creates a public for the article.

WikiProjects are focused on coordinating the work of groups of editors who collaborate on specific article collections. A degree in politics is not required in order to be part of WikiProject: Politics. Membership is granted the moment a user lists themselves as part of the project and signs up for notifications.

Although there is a large backlog of new articles on Wikipedia, they don't have to be dealt with in the order that they are received. Editors reviewing new articles can select which ones they want to work on. So, after creating the article, The Egyptian Liberal immediately sets about trying to obtain support from other editors. He knows that the next hours are critical for the survival of the article, and the immediate goal is for another editor to approve its existence.

A few minutes after he publishes the first version of the article, he posts a request for help on the user page of Lihaas, a Wikipedian whom he has worked with on other articles over the past few months. "We need to finish this page ASAP and then we can set it up for ITN [In the news], or alternatively DYK [Did you know?]"[14]

The "In the news" and "Did you know?" sections are featured on Wikipedia's main landing pages. They are human-curated lists of what Wikipedians working on the sections believe are the most relevant articles at particular points in time but will only be linked when they have met a standard of quality necessary for being displayed at this top spot. In referencing English Wikipedia's main page, The Egyptian Liberal highlights what he sees as the key destination for the facts that he is setting out in the 2011 Egyptian protests article. English Wikipedia consists of more than six million articles. A link to the article that he has started on one of the site's most visited pages is a valued destination.

Wikipedia's home page in English, then, is established early on as a key destination for facts by its first author. To catalyze this travel, the article will need to reach a standard of quality that justifies the attention that would inevitably result from this focus. Many more editors will have to join him to enable this improvement. Many will have to summarize rapidly multiplying sources and continually condense those statements to reflect current events.

In the end, the editor who reviews the article is neither Lihaas nor someone notified from the portals or projects where it was automatically listed. A couple of hours after the article is created, English Wikipedia user Heroeswithmetaphors discovers it after reading a BBC story about the protests and going to English Wikipedia to find out more.

Heroeswithmetaphors is an American Wikipedia editor, editing since 2006 and living in Buenos Aires, Argentina. We chatted about the article directly on our Wikipedia talk pages—with me blundering about as I tried to conduct an interview in the open on my talk pages, worrying about whether my questions were too publicly intrusive (who are you? what is your gender?), and him responding promptly and politely but giving nothing intimate away.

Heroeswithmetaphors' critical work on the article demonstrates a distinguishing feature of Wikipedians. After discovering new information from sources outside of Wikipedia, Wikipedians will immediately check whether that information is reflected on Wikipedia and will add it if it isn't. Whereas others might merely stop their search when they see missing information in the repository or look elsewhere, Wikipedians will take action. That step (from inaction to action)—what motivates it, what is required to catalyze it, why it tends to be located in particular demographics—is something that plagues researchers and Wikipedia activists in their quest to grow the active editor base of the encyclopedia. What makes someone click on the edit button of an article in order to update or question the facts that it contains? Is it because you care about free knowledge, because you live in North America, because you are a man, or because you have free time?

In this case, Heroeswithmetaphors is at least partly driven by a belief that what is happening in Egypt (as verified by the BBC story) is significant. He removes the article's "new unreviewed article" tag, thus accepting the new article into the repository. Heroeswithmetaphors continues to edit the article over the next few hours, fixing some of the grammar, adding relevant links and categories, adding another sentence about the "unprecedented" nature of the protests, citing the *Christian Science Monitor*, and fixing the formatting of references in the article.

He notices that the article is being sourced to "bare URLs" (without details of authors, source titles, and dates), and he is concerned that novice editors who take the same route as he did (from traditional media to Wikipedia) will start to edit the article without filling in the important metadata for each source, including the work's title, author, and date. Such metadata is important for fulfilling the verifiability criteria of Wikipedia since URLs can change and become inaccessible, and detailed information about sources on Wikipedia is important for users to be able to check where information is coming from.

Heroeswithmetaphors goes to the (currently blank) talk page of the article and makes an announcement for editors about referencing as he continues to fix citations by adding metadata to them. "(W)e will have a lot of novice editors coming here soon, so let's make sure to properly format references,"[15] he writes. Heroeswithmetaphors will go on to work on other articles shortly after this, but he has played a significant role in accepting the 2011 Egyptian protests article into Wikipedia's repository and has stabilized it to some extent against possible attacks.

DOCUMENTING THE FUTURE

What stands out from the first version of the article is the rapid movement between the past and the future. The future leaps from the page, creating a disjuncture from what is expected from an encyclopedic article. Instead of talking about events as they have taken place, for example, the article jumps between past and present tense. The lead text starts in the present tense: "The 2011 Egyptian protests *are* a continuing series of street demonstrations taking place throughout Egypt." This is followed by a sentence written in the past tense: "The demonstrations and riots *were* reported to have started . . ." (my emphases).

The future is also signaled by the word "ongoing" as the value for the end date field in the infobox of the event, and the cartoon image predicts a future in which the people (represented by Khaled Mohamed Saeed) rise up to quash the "tiny, flailing" Hosni Mubarak. The news source cited in the article is written as a report about the (future) plan for the protests rather than as a report on the protests themselves.

By creating a new article about events before they have even begun, The Egyptian Liberal is effectively setting up a space to document the future. Facts are not only born digital. They are immediately constituted by data and code. Facts are represented by data including the event's start and end dates in the infobox and the event's categories. They are enclosed by code that enables different velocity for facts to travel. The process of article creation about breaking news events is future oriented. Wikipedians' use of code serves this purpose by stabilizing unstable facts and by laying down possible avenues along which facts may travel.

STABILIZING UNSTABLE FACTS

To a seasoned Wikipedian, the addition of particular objects or elements to an article is essential to the successful travel of facts contained within it. Like the previous century's printer's trays fitted with specially constructed lead letters and punctuation marks for the printing of newspapers and books, Wikipedia articles have limited possibilities for representation. A blank wiki page is certainly not as inflexible as a wooden or leaden printer's tray. It can technically exclude certain objects or be dominated by one or two elements, but Wikipedia articles are much more likely to survive and thrive if they are constructed in the form and style that have grown out of Wikipedia practice.

The process of stabilization on Wikipedia requires both a literal explanation of the event and its importance and also a material rooting of the article into the terrain in which facts will travel. Such rooting practically requires that The Egyptian Liberal insert as many hyperlinks as possible into the article, linking the article to other Wikipedia articles and categories (to establish relevance) and to external sources of information (in order to establish significance). Like tent pegs pushed into the ground to keep a tent in place, hyperlinks serve to root the article into the infrastructures of Wikipedia and the web.

Hyperlinks to Wikipedia articles and categories serve to frame the article as relevant to the entire collection. This is of such importance that

Wikipedians have special terms for articles without any incoming links from other Wikipedia pages: they are "orphaned" or "lonely" or "pages with no parent." There is even a WikiProject called Project Orphanage,[16] with the goal of clearing up the backlog of orphaned articles. Without being referred to by other pages, an article tagged as an orphan could be seen as non-noteworthy and deleted.

Outgoing hyperlinks or citations to external sources are essential for meeting Wikipedia's verifiability requirements. When articles with no citations are published on English Wikipedia, they are automatically flagged and added to a number of watch lists. In the New Pages Feed, for example, where new articles are evaluated, articles with no citations are flagged with the "no citation" tag. When I asked The Egyptian Liberal if the article had been nominated for deletion, he replied that he "had enough sources there, so nobody [could] claim that there weren't enough sources [indicating that] it was a significant event."[17]

Terms in the lead section and links to articles for further reading (both within and outside of Wikipedia) serve to connect the unstable phenomena in Egypt to more stable phenomena. This is achieved through hyperlinking to articles about "unemployment" (created in 2001), to further reading in the article titled "2010–2011 Tunisian Protests," and to categories such as "Protest marches," which contain lists of articles.

Facts at this stage of an event are thin on the ground, and analysis of those facts is even thinner. Connecting the event to related, more secure events provides a sense of steadiness and firmness by association. Hyperlinks are served by their material code but also by their symbolic associations.

LAYING OUT POSSIBILITIES

The second key function of code in the context of article creation is to lay out the possibilities for the future travel of facts within the Wikimedia universe and the web more generally. When articles are created, facts are embedded in objects like the title, lead, infobox, and categories. Each of these objects is enlivened by code that determines how facts are represented on the page, but also by the future possibilities for how those objects might travel beyond the article space.

Objects are coded differently—their possibilities for future travel are not equal. Rules about who can alter the contents of the objects, as well as the shape of the objects themselves, are instrumental to the possibilities that will influence fact travel. So, too, is the extent to which code marks the boundaries of facts contained within those objects.

Infoboxes, remember, are coded so that each pair in the box ("location: Egypt," for example) can be easily targeted, extracted, and used to populate other websites. The code that wraps around these pairs (called key-value-pairs) in the infobox determines that the key facts about events can be easily extracted separately from other facts in the article.

The effect of the addition of code, or the code wrapping facts and objects in the article, is to make some facts lighter or heavier than others. Facts in the infobox become lighter and easier to move at scale because their values are predetermined and abstracted across a range of other articles. The first paragraph of Wikipedia articles is similarly targeted by algorithms for defining phenomena by question-and-answer machines like Apple's Siri and Google's knowledge panels. The first paragraphs have similar potential for travel, but facts further down in the article are heavier and more immovable.

Each object in the article serves to classify the article, to establish the meaning of what happened, and to note why this represents a significant break from the past. In so doing, the article defines possible routes for travel of the facts contained within it. Each object is coded according to particular rules and conventions. The facts contained within them are brimming with meaning that will help us understand what happened and why it happened now, rather than before or after. Each object contains different possibilities for the travel of facts within it—if the article can just remain in the database long enough to gain traction.

"THINGS THAT HAVEN'T EVEN STOPPED HAPPENING YET"

In the words of *New York Times* columnist Jonathan Dee, "Wikipedia's notion of the past has enlarged to include things that haven't even stopped happening yet."[18] In covering events before their meaning has stabilized, Wikipedians play an active role not only in telling the (hi)story of events but in determining how those events will play out.

It is not insignificant that this meaning making is happening on an encyclopedia rather than a newspaper or blog. In writing about events in their very early stages, The Egyptian Liberal is attempting to fit the very unstable facts about the event into the stable, authoritative, encyclopedic form in this unique melding of the journalistic and encyclopedic forms. His role as frame maker is critical for the future retelling of events. An early quantitative study of Wikipedia articles over time noted that there is a "first mover advantage on Wikipedia."[19] By visualizing the ways in which articles evolved over time and the survival rate of article text over time, Fernanda Viégas, Martin Wattenberg, and Dave Kushal found that "the initial text of a page tends to survive longer and tends to suffer fewer modifications than later contributions to the same page." The authors hypothesized that "the first person to create a page generally sets the tone of the article on that page and, therefore, their text usually has the highest survival rate."

Zooming in on the first edits of the article, we can see qualitatively what constitutes the "tone" of the article, with all its embedded symbols, classifications, and associations. The Egyptian Liberal creates the article in order to establish a defensive position and with his own hopes and dreams for the event deeply embedded. The implications are that The Egyptian Liberal actively creates as much as he passively reflects what is happening in Egypt.

January 25, the so-called Day of Rage, leaves three people dead, and officials state that more than twenty people have been arrested in Cairo. What will happen next is an unknown. The protests could be violently quashed by security forces, as has happened in the past. But the spark of a revolution has been lit, and the possibilities for what could happen over the next few days are potentially groundbreaking.

Similarly, on Wikipedia, The Egyptian Liberal creates his own spark, but just as in the events themselves, other editors must join him in a full detonation of the event in order for the narrative (and the events carried with it) to be sustained.

Inevitably, given the demographics of English Wikipedia, the editors who will determine the success of the article will come from North America and Western Europe. It is these editors who need to be convinced of the event's significance, as well as The Egyptian Liberal's suggested labeling of the event's victims, perpetrators, and legitimate witnesses.

4

ESCALATION

MISSION CONTROL: ADVERSARIAL COLLABORATION

Thousands of protesters take to the streets of Egypt the next day (January 26). The widespread disorder is covered by major news agencies around the world. The Arabic Wikipedian عمرو:مستخدم or Amr has created the Arabic version of the article (titled "Day of Rage" in Arabic), published about three hours after the English version.[1] A few hours later The Egyptian Liberal changes (or moves, in Wikipedia terminology) the article's title to "2011 Egyptian Revolution." A few hours after that, Mohamed Ouda changes the title yet again to "Protests in Egypt 2011." It will face multiple name changes in the days to come.

After the first twenty-four hours of the life of the English Wikipedia article, forty-two editors have joined The Egyptian Liberal and the article has been edited 130 times. It has grown in size (now 18 kilobytes and about 1,300 words) as editors iteratively add facts as they are reported in local and international media.

Editors (some of whom have worked together on other articles before this) quickly settle into a routine. After twenty-four hours there have been almost two hundred edits to the article and two hundred different versions of the article have been produced. The Egyptian Liberal is by far the most prolific editor at this stage, but on day four of the protests, the editor Ocaasi starts editing the article and soon assumes unofficial leadership over the page in partnership with The Egyptian Liberal.

Ocaasi is Jake Orlowitz, an American who was twenty-eight when the protests started in Egypt. He had recently graduated with a college degree in philosophy, economics, history, and social theory in Connecticut and had moved back home in the US. In one of my many interviews with him, Ocaasi said that his collaboration with The Egyptian Liberal was productive because of their different vantage points. "We developed a highly symbiotic relationship. The Egyptian Liberal knew who was important in Egypt. He had the connections while I had the ability to research and write particularly well in English."[2]

Ocaasi was suffering from anxiety and agoraphobia at the time, but 2011 was a turning point.[3] He was in the house all day and all night, socially isolated but editing Wikipedia obsessively. In an interview with him at a Wikipedia gathering in Vienna in 2017, Ocaasi told me that 2011 was a galvanizing moment for him.

> Everything before that on Wikipedia was just playing around and this was not. It was also when my innocence about Wikipedia ended. It wasn't just a hobby or escape. . . . I was connected to this real knowledge ecosystem. . . . There were hundreds of thousands of people reading [the article] and I knew that. There was a profound sense of responsibility. . . . I thought the world mattered so much those days and I thought I could play a part—not in an activist sense but by documenting what was happening.[4]

One might imagine that coordination isn't necessary for work on a wiki when every new editor merely assesses what is in the article and edits it to fill any gaps. But there are three main reasons why coordination is critical, especially when writing about high-volume news events.

The first is that sources are multiplying and the events themselves are evolving swiftly. Rather than simply adding facts as single sources announce changes, editors need to coordinate with one another to ensure that the latest developments can be verified by multiple reliable sources.

Second is that editors need to develop local agreement at the article level about what constitutes reliable sources in the context of the event. If sources commonly recognized as reliable in the context of English Wikipedia are not available, then consensus will have to be found to determine alternative sources as reliable.

And third is that editors (both new and experienced) require common knowledge in order to work together on the article. For new editors, that knowledge is primarily centered on Wikipedia's policies. Experienced editors will need to know critical information about the geographic region in which events are occurring to establish common standards.

In the context of this article, the number of active Wikipedians in Egypt is relatively low, and the number of Egyptian Wikipedians who are able to edit English Wikipedia is even lower given that English is not natively spoken in Egypt. Articles relating to breaking news events always result in an influx of editors new to Wikipedia who need to be educated about Wikipedia's policies and norms. Even among experienced editors, work will need to be done to develop consistency in the spelling of names and terms originally in Arabic and brokering work done to license images for use on Wikipedia if Wikipedians are not available to take high-quality photos that can be used in the article.

Inexperienced editors make a significant contribution to the article, but a small percentage of editors undertake formatting and coordination tasks that take up the majority of edits. Coordination tasks include making regular announcements about the state of the article, providing lists of tasks for others to work on, responding to requests for edits on the talk pages, and intervening in conflicts between editors.

Although Ocaasi and The Egyptian Liberal handle most of the work on the page, they are by no means the only ones coordinating tasks. Silver seren, for example, adds new information and sources according to recent events on the talk page. An American university student at the time, Silver seren has a deep knowledge of Wikipedia's reliable sources policy and assumes the task of selecting sources that he believes are acceptable under that policy. The growing number of sources and their summaries serve both as a running list of tasks for keeping the article up to date and as a demonstration to other editors about what types of sources are considered reliable. Editors check off Silver seren's sources after they have added relevant information to the article. Silver seren acts as a kind of librarian, tracking breaking news from reliable sources, which is particularly useful given his experience with what English Wikipedia considers reliable.

License broker Aude is a seasoned Wikipedian from the United States. She becomes central to the development of the article because she has lived in Egypt and has knowledge of the political context there as well as local contacts. Aude maintains a list of reliable sources on her talk page throughout the protests. She contributes to debates and takes the lead in sourcing images for use on the page.

Early in the protests, editors are having a hard time finding openly licensed photographs of the demonstrations. Aude writes that she is in contact with Al Jazeera—the Qatari, state-funded news agency—to license images and videos under the Creative Commons Attribution Share-Alike license, which is vital if they are to be used on Wikipedia. Aude plays a critical role in ensuring that there are good-quality images and video of the protests by facilitating the licensing of images and video using Creative Commons and finding help in converting videos into the open source "ogg" format.

Lihaas, too, makes significant contributions to the talk pages and is a frequent editor of the article. By January 29, Lihaas has made over 150 edits to the article.

Many of the editors are avidly watching the live feed of events on Al Jazeera television or online via Al Jazeera's YouTube channel as they edit, and they work in informal shifts in order to cover events as they progress. The talk page becomes a kind of mission control, where editors alert one another about breaking news, request help in adding sources, point out flaws or weaknesses on the page, propose edits, and request that other editors make changes or additions to the article.

Editors use the talk page to coordinate work. They explain the edit they just made if it responds to something that has just happened or if they believe the edit might be contentious. They direct attention to where they have either added a fact because new information has become available or removed a fact because they believe that it goes against Wikipedia's policies. The Egyptian Liberal, for example, asks that editors stop removing a statement in the article because he says that it is accurate (it was "taken from a New York Times article"). Others explain why they have removed information that is unsourced or does not reflect Wikipedia's NPOV policy.

Although editors could provide these explanations in an "edit summary" that they fill in while making edits, they often prefer the talk page because it affords much richer communication than is available in the stream of edits in the history database. The article space contains much excitement at this stage, and editors find opportunities to connect with one another: on the article's talk page, on their own talk pages, and even on platforms outside Wikipedia, such as email and social media.

Editors also use the talk page to brainstorm ideas on how to organize the material in the article by proposing changes and requesting feedback or alternative suggestions before they make the changes. Editing the lead paragraph of the article requires a high degree of coordination because it is in this paragraph that the entire event is summarized. Inevitably, other editors' work will need to be erased in the significant overhauls required by this process.

In one of my interviews with Ocaasi, he said that it was like being "an emergency doctor for the first week or so. As the pace got calmer, the edits got bigger. [I was making] structural changes, structuring the page . . . moving things while it was being so heavily edited." Ocaasi recalled that this meant that "edit conflict was guaranteed." He knew that by making larger structural changes he was going to write over someone's work. "Someone needed to make those big changes and be committed enough for fixing things that they had stepped over."[5]

On January 28, for example, Ocaasi uses the talk page to show his "rough attempt" at summarizing the lead and asks for feedback. Ten hours later, Silver seren replies with a new draft, writing that he has "attacked [the] draft with commas" and suggests adding sentences about the internet and cellphone blackout. Summarizing the lead to accurately reflect the entire article means not overemphasizing small details or attributing positions inaccurately. Reorganizing the article to remove material or moving material to other articles requires significant intensive work, expertise, and knowledge of the article. Significant changes like this are unlikely to be sustained unless those whose material is being removed have been consulted.

Less onerous tasks include checking whether the sources are being accurately summarized in the text of the article, or whether the facts are indeed supported by their attendant citations. On January 28, for example, BazaNews writes that news about Mubarak's family fleeing should be removed because the article from which it is sourced "says that it is false." The work of verifying whether the sources displayed are accurately reflected in their summaries in the article is a common task of

Wikipedians, even though sometimes, when multiple sources are streaming into the article, false information can remain for long periods.

Other editors expand on events through the accretion of facts. Wikipedia's coverage of events often includes an "international reactions" section where editors add single sentences summarizing stories about national leaders' reactions to events. This kind of information is easily reviewed and added to by individual editors without having to alter existing material.

In addition to the work of human editors, bots do regular work in preventing vandalism and correcting references. Three of the most active bots that edit the article are ClueBot NG, a vandalism detection bot; SmackBot, which corrects ISBNs, among other editorial tasks; and AnomieBOT, which corrects pages with incorrect reference formatting and performs other tasks. ClueBot NG works by developing an algorithmic portrait of what vandalistic content looks like and applying rules (as well as its experience of detecting vandalism before this event) in order to determine what content is valid. On January 28, for example, ClueBot reverts an edit by an anonymous editor (with an IP address in California) in which the phrase "ALLAHU AKBAR"[6] was added in the lead sentence of the article. The IP's edit doesn't last more than a few seconds before it is caught and automatically reverted.[7]

GETTING TO THE SOURCE

Once the article has been approved, there is some reprieve, but its existence can still be challenged at any point. To retain its status as a legitimate host of facts on Wikipedia, it needs to attract multiple allies and traveling companions, in the form of editors, sources, and readers. Because opposition to facts fuels attention and labor, facts' editorial allies include not only those who support the facts' representation on Wikipedia but also those who dispute it.

In the birth stage of the article, good allies are experienced editors who recognize the significance or notability of the article; at the next stage, good allies are those that come in scale. A large volume of editors working on various aspects of the article, as well as diversity in their makeup, is critical. So, too, is a steady stream of external sources covering the events. Also essential at this stage is an even larger number of readers of the article who accept Wikipedia's recognition of the events as important and turn their attention to the site as a source for breaking news.

A massive crowd moves into the article, led by a team that coalesces around common tasks. What is needed is for attention on the events to be sustained—not only on Wikipedia but in the sources that it depends on to feed its machinery. Facts need a constant supply of traveling companions in order to sustain the event's historic status. This practice on Wikipedia mirrors what is happening on the ground in Egypt. The catalyst for the event requires the participation of key actors who understand how to shape their messages in ways that will ignite popular participation. For attention on the event to be sustained, the public will need to continue to fill the streets in large numbers and maintain their focus on the common goal of bringing down Mubarak's government. Publics outside the event's epicenter in Egypt will also need to pay attention to the event.

During breaking news events, editors use sources as a way to verify claims being made, and their citations as a trail for users to follow in order to verify whether the sources are being accurately reflected. The discovery, triangulation, selection, and summarizing of sources are central to the practice of article editing, and sourcing practice plays an important role in determining which sources are more prominently displayed than others. The ways in which editors compile facts in the article, using particular types of sources and citing a subset of those sources, work to frame the article in particular ways. The article starts to fill with accumulated facts, all with their attendant traveling companions. Sometimes those companions do battle when there are competing alternative claims.

If Wikipedia is built on the principle that every statement, especially potentially controversial statements, should be backed up by a reliable source, then a good way of understanding how Wikipedia's articles are shaped is to look at where its sources come from.

In 2012, I connected with two data scientists, David Musicant and Shilad Sen, who were also interested in studying Wikipedia sources.[8] Our findings suggested the rise of new influential sources of information on the web. Analyzing eleven million sources on English Wikipedia, we found that American publishers dominated, with the largest proportion of sources originating from traditional news media. We also discovered that a significant proportion were from government information sources and from organizations and individuals producing statistics and data. This was interesting because it demonstrated that while Wikipedia policy on reliable sources clearly indicates a preference for peer-reviewed, scholarly sources of information, there is a practice favoring quite different sources.

We evaluated articles across the encyclopedia, but the problem was that, across different topics, articles varied in their dynamics. Two years later, in a project led by Shilad Sen, we worked with Brent Hecht, Oliver Keyes, and Mark Graham to investigate how "local" Wikipedia articles about places were.[9] In other words, to what extent did articles about places use sources from those places? And to what extent were editors writing about that place from that place?

We did this by analyzing the locations of sources and of editors across articles about places in multiple language versions of the encyclopedia, a characteristic we called "geoprovenance." First, we studied where editors working on articles about places were located. Second, we studied the locations of publishers of sources cited in articles about places. We found that articles about places written in countries that natively speak the language of the Wikipedia edition (articles about Iraq for the Arabic Wikipedia, for example) were more than five times more likely to have local content than for content about places that were written in a language that was non-native. Access to broadband also played an important role in editor localness, and countries with a small scholarly publishing network produced substantially fewer sources. Countries with few native speakers of a particular Wikipedia language edition produced far fewer editors. Our conclusion was that if a place faces serious socioeconomic obstacles, or if you read about a place in a language that is not spoken in that place, you are unlikely to be reading locally produced content, or content that references local sources.

When I started analyzing the Egyptian protests article, my thinking about sources changed radically. Our earlier studies analyzing articles about places on Wikipedia suggested that the Arabic version of the article would contain a majority of Egyptian sources and the English version would contain predominantly English-language sources, chiefly from the United States. But I discovered that the sources dominant in the English version were not from the United States or the United Kingdom and that the Arabic version of the article did not rely on Egyptian publishers.

CITED SOURCES: THE RISE OF AL JAZEERA

Modern Standard Arabic is the official language of Egypt. As mentioned earlier, the Arabic Wikipedia article about the events in Egypt is started by the editor Amr about three hours after the English version. After twenty-four hours of editing, the Arabic version contains four references, while the English version contains twenty-nine. On Arabic Wikipedia, only one source is Egyptian: *Al Dostor*, an independent opposition newspaper. The other sources are BBC Arabic and Al Arabia, a Saudi free-to-air television news channel. The English version of the article contains primarily traditional news sources but also includes citations to a blog, a legal text, and a nongovernmental organization (NGO).

Just over two weeks later (in the final English Wikipedia version on February 10, 2011) the article contains 371 citations. The majority are in English, but about 6 percent are in Arabic. Eighty-five percent of the citations are from traditional media sources, but there are about 2 percent each from NGOs, think tanks, blogs, and social media. A further 2 percent are from sources trying to hijack the article for advertising or to manipulate search engine rankings.

Al Jazeera is the dominant source in the Egyptian protests article, accounting for almost 20 percent (or sixty-eight) of all citations. Reuters, the BBC, the *New York Times*, the Associated Press, and the *Guardian* trail behind Al Jazeera, accounting for around 5 percent each (or eighteen) of the almost four hundred citations. The majority of the sources are used only once or twice. Regional coverage other than from Al Jazeera is limited to three sources. Two are from Israel: *Haaretz* and Ynet; a third is to Al Arabiya. The only Egyptian source is *Al-Masry Al-Youm*, a privately owned daily newspaper, with about 4 percent (or fourteen) of citations.

English-language sources from outside Egypt are prevalent in the article, but US and British sources are not as central as they were in our earlier studies. Instead, Al Jazeera dominates the sources used by English Wikipedia editors. The *New York Times*, for example, which was the second most popular source in our study of all English Wikipedia sources, comes in a distant fourth after two weeks of protest in Egypt.

The Egyptian revolution signaled an important moment in Al Jazeera's global rise to prominence,[10] especially in the United States, where it had been banned by cable television companies and declared as anti-American during the Iraq War. In the first days of the protests, the Al Jazeera English website saw an increase in traffic by 2,500 percent, 60 percent of which originated from the United States, as it livestreamed events from Egypt.[11] News reports at the time indicated that the US government was paying attention to Al Jazeera and that US State Department officials, including Hillary Clinton, commented that Al Jazeera was providing "real" news that US stations were failing to deliver.[12]

In numerous ways, Al Jazeera suited the format, practices, and policies of Wikipedia in the early stages of the article's development. Coverage by Al Jazeera was unique because it was live, round-the-clock, and featured up-close images that other news agencies did not have access to. According to a *New York Times* report, "While American television networks were scrambling to move reporters and producers into Cairo, the Al Jazeera channels were already there."[13] Americans, the highest proportion of Wikipedia English editors, were particularly captivated by Al Jazeera's coverage. Al Jazeera agreed to license their images under a Creative Commons license that would be compatible with their being published on Wikipedia.

Al Jazeera met the high demand for news from Egypt. The Egyptian protests became one of the biggest news stories of the year in the United States. The Pew Research Center, for example, found that coverage of the Egyptian unrest between January 31 and February 6 "registered as the biggest international story in the past four years—surpassing any coverage of the Iraq war, the Haiti earthquake, and the conflict in Afghanistan."[14]

Although editors on English Wikipedia did not widely agree on Al Jazeera as a reliable source before the Arab Spring, a number of editors of the Egyptian revolution article noted that the media channel gained this status by providing regular, accessible accounts in both broadcasting and textual formats during the protests. According to Ocaasi, Al Jazeera was "leading the breaking news [and] would be the first to report news stories on the website using footage as well as textual analysis, and a live blog providing short textual analysis of events as they happened."[15]

When editors make statements on the talk page of the article affirming Al Jazeera as a reliable source, other editors do not oppose them, and Al Jazeera stories are regularly cited on the talk page when editors update one another about what is happening on the ground in Egypt. On February 6, for example, Lihaas's edits claiming that Mubarak had resigned from his party are reverted by another user. Lihaas opposes the reversion by stating that "al jazeera (which has been unanimously declared a fair source above) mention[s] his resignation."

But there is no evidence of Al Jazeera being "unanimously declared a fair source" according to collective decision-making, either at the level of the article or in the encyclopedia as a whole. Wikipedians like Lihaas were making decisions about what constituted a reliable source through claims like the one above, and Al Jazeera became a reliable source by virtue of the fact that opposition to its inclusion faded over time.

Documenting an evolving event on an encyclopedia inevitably reflects tensions between practical and theoretical verifiability. Theoretically, verifiability demands that Wikipedia's readers be able to discover the source of each claim in order to verify its accuracy or inaccuracy. But there are multiple occasions in which the reference provided for a statement is not its true source, its true companion. Summarizing a source or declaring that a sentence is derived from a particular source does not necessarily mean that it has been accurately reflected. Sometimes, editors append a citation to a sentence that bears little resemblance to the arguments in the source. Often, these problems go unnoticed since it requires time and effort for editors to read the entire text from which statements are supposedly sourced, and there are often multiple sources for each statement.

In theory, sources are good traveling companions only when editors are able to follow the source in order to evaluate its quality and the extent to which it has been accurately summarized. But in practice, sources are popular on Wikipedia when they fit the contexts of editing and what editors perceive will be most acceptable given their options when events are evolving rapidly, rather than whether they are examples of quality sources according to Wikipedia policy. In the wider context of Wikipedia's coverage of historic events, sources that are most useful are accessible under the conditions of editing and practical for those without an already deep knowledge of the subject.

Editors are unlikely to have the time to read lengthy academic texts about Egypt, and the timelines for academics publishing work relating to current events do not favor the rapid collation of modular facts in the wake of a historic event. Instead, Wikipedians use live footage and up-to-the-minute journalistic reports, supported by a network of journalists and citizen journalists tweeting, live blogging, and providing regular alerts across a number of news channels.

For Wikipedians working on the developing article, the most accessible sources are those that are written in English, written for popular audiences, and either free (rather than behind a paywall) or openly licensed (in the case of images). Accessibility, then, relates to both the style of texts (for use by nonacademic audiences) and their availability at no cost. The latter becomes doubly important for Wikipedians given the verifiability requirement, which means that even if editors can access sources behind paywalls, their readers may not be able to.

Since readers should be able to verify information that they read, the trend is toward the use of textual, open access sources written in English. Social media sources and television sources are difficult to cite in ways that would enable readers and other editors to continually verify the information they represent. A hyperlink to a textual source is ideal in terms of verifiability, and so social media and televised sources tend to be replaced by journalistic articles.

As a result of these trends, we see the rise of journalistic sources (particularly Al Jazeera English) written in English, and a minimal presence of academic and scientific sources. Before the protests, the Egyptian government believed that it controlled the local media. But the government's perspective was almost completely absent in the early stages of the protests (other than statements from officials broadcast by state television).

Protesters dominated coverage of events because Westerners covering the events were accessing sources in which government representatives were absent. (The fact that many Wikipedians identified with the protesters given their mutual disrespect for authoritarianism, and the alignment with American democratic principles, was equally important in this choice.) As a result, the protesters' narrative dominates the account.

HIDDEN SOURCES AND TRUE COMPANIONS

As I interviewed editors about their editing practices over the years, I became more convinced that I needed to look beyond cited sources in order to understand Wikipedia's true sources of information. Looking only at the citations in an article as the source of its shaping is problematic because it takes for granted Wikipedia's claim that it is merely passively summarizing what already exists in "reliable sources." But Wikipedians are actively participating in the events that they are describing, not least of which involves deciding what constitutes a reliable source at the point of inclusion.

The true sources of the historical narrative, I learned, derive from the information-seeking practices editors are engaged in and editors' experiences as witnesses to the event. Explicitly cited sources are just the tip of the iceberg in discovering the source of Wikipedia's accounts of the world. Getting to the true source of information in the article requires not only taking account of the kinds of citations that Wikipedia editors were adding and removing, but also analyzing the discussions with editors about their sourcing practices and interviewing them about how they were experiencing the event at the time.

The sources that dominate the article demonstrate how Wikipedians' practice in editing fast-moving events of global importance taking place outside of the English-speaking world lead to very different types of sources being chosen. Wikipedians themselves are critical sources of information in the article, and they actively construct the events that they describe because they are witnesses to historic events—either within the local epicenter or by virtue of their watching broadcasts of events on television or online.

Studying the Egyptian protests article, I discovered that editors perform three knowledge-building practices that point to sources other than citations being used as the foundation of the article.

First, editing practice in the context of historic events demonstrates the continued importance of broadcasting as the original source of news in many cases, and search engines in surfacing sources that are ultimately cited. Search engines are actually a key source of information, not only because their automated ranking of results for users' queries determine which sources will be selected, but also because services like Google Trends are used, for example, in calculating the relative proportion of different views in the public domain when deciding on naming conventions.

Second, although social media sources—particularly Facebook, Twitter, and YouTube—may be critical sources for events, they will be iteratively removed from the article over time. This is because Wikipedia's policy warns against the use of social media as reliable sources and because social media sources are materially fragile, often removed, and difficult to archive.

Third, although Wikipedia forbids "original research," the local and contextual knowledge provided by Wikipedians themselves are critical to the successful development of the article. Wikipedians are constantly applying their own experience and knowledge of a phenomenon when selecting sources and summarizing them. This is especially relevant in the context of current events because every editor is experiencing the event as a witness to history while also attempting to document it. Editors become enrolled as witnesses by experiencing events as they evolve across mediated forms and are actively participating in their narration. This is yet another reason why documenting events as they happen on Wikipedia is very different from documenting an event that happened before an editor's lifetime or one that lay beyond the bounds of their experience.

GOOGLE AS A GATEWAY TO (TEXTUAL) SOURCE DISCOVERY

Many of the editors I interviewed about the article noted that their editing processes began with watching live video of what was happening on the ground; then they used Google to search for alternative (or additional) sources of information for the article. Video sources are difficult to cite because they are not always archived. When they are archived, editors must be able to discover where the live footage is housed. Waiting for video archives to be edited and published, and then finding the same footage they watched is too time-consuming for the rapid pace of editing required by a breaking news article. Instead, inspired by what they are witnessing in the broadcast news, many editors use Google News search to discover textual news stories to read and cite.

Although never cited, Google News, then, becomes an important source for breaking news about the event and for gauging the popularity of different terms. Ocaasi, for example, noted in one of my interviews with him that he was regularly watching Al Jazeera English's live television coverage and used Google to find stories in online newspapers when new events were flagged by the live coverage:

> There were different streams of immediacy . . . well, I was one of them just glued to Al Jazeera's live feed from Tahrir Square, and so I was watching that

and then when they would say something new, then I would go and look for whether or not Associated Press or *New York Times* had run with anything. . . . So I would kind of use the breaking news television as inspiration to go find sources and then at the same time I was just scouring Google News for the information coming in about the Egyptian Revolution.[16]

In addition to using Google's algorithm to surface new sources, editors also use Google as evidence to support bids for changing the naming and categorization of the events in Egypt. News sources, political authorities, and protest groups use different names for events as they unfold, and some protest groups offer a different title for each day of the protests: January 28, for example, is called "Friday of Anger" by some and "Day of Rage" by others, but the latter title is also used for the first protests on January 25. The article was created with the title "2011 Egyptian Protests," but after a few days some editors call for changing the term "protests" to either "uprising" or "revolution." In response, Ocaasi uses Google News numbers to indicate the relative popularity of different terms:

Just a rough guide, Google News search limited to the past 7 days for Egypt protests: *27,693*; for Egypt uprising: *11,305* (note: similar breakdown of about 2.5:1 for egyptian protests, egyptian uprising). See also Google Trends (egypt protests, egypt uprising) [1]. And check out the Google Trends regional breakout at the bottom, where the "uprising" term has indeed caught on more in the US than the UK or Canada.[17]

Other editors, including Lothar von Richthofen and Userpd, provide links to Google News searches for the alternative terms as evidence of opposition or support, but Cs32en counters that editors should look at how reliable sources have been using titles in their reports rather than looking at numbers that simply add up *all* occurrences, regardless of their reliability: "[A] Google search can't really answer the question of whether *the movement as a whole* is being seen as an uprising, a revolution, a revolt, or as (a number of) protests. We have to look carefully at the context in which reliable sources use words such as 'protests' or 'uprising'."[18]

But Cs32en's comments seem to contradict one another: should reliable sources be prioritized in deciding how "the movement as a whole" is being seen? Which sources are most reliable in this context? Journalists? Governments? The protesters themselves? Especially in the early days of the protests, sources that were traditionally held up as most reliable on English

Wikipedia (the BBC, the *New York Times*, and the *Guardian*) were caught unawares, with few of their own journalists on the ground in Egypt to report on events. This vacuum was filled by sources that many English Wikipedians found difficult to evaluate.

In the comment below, Userpd opposes one editor's suggestion that the article title be changed from "protests" to "uprising." Userpd discredits the nominator by declaring that the nominator is biased (the editor is "known for his pro-right Israeli edits," implying that it is in Israel's best interests to discredit the protesters). Instead, Userpd favors Russian sources, which have been calling the events "protests" from "the beginning."

In other sources in different languages the word "Protest" (was used from the beginning), for example russian ones: gazeta.ru, lenta.ru, 1 state channel, Russia. So I think we can manage without this cliche / label from mainly pro-right Israeli side.[19]

Silver seren responds with his own interpretation of Russian sources, asserting that it is actually in the *Russian* media's best interests to call events in Egypt a protest rather than an uprising because they fear similar actions by "former bloc countries."

As for Russia, [I]'m not sure what you're expecting to find there. Of course they don't use the term Uprising. That is a term that Russian media does not want to go throwing around. Russia might not be being as extravagantly censorist as China is, but they are still being careful of what they say. Not that Russia has to worry about that as much from the main population, they love Russia, but more from the outlying territories, the former bloc countries. Believe me, I know how Russia works. Go read my article on the War of Laws.[20]

Events in Egypt have attracted global attention, and national interests outside of Egypt indicate an investment in opposing outcomes. Wikipedia editors find it difficult to navigate among the national media sources they are either unfamiliar with or where there are radically different opinions about their potential biases, depending on editors' identities, past experiences, and knowledges. There are no simple, quick methods for determining which sources should be prioritized in the naming of events or for balancing names against one another. As a result, they use what is available to them, calculating the numerical weight of each title according to Google.

Google, consequently, becomes an obligatory passage point in the construction of the article, both because editors use Google News to search for updates for what's happening and to corroborate or refute evidence found elsewhere, and because Google Trends is used as a source for deciding changes to the titles of events.

SOCIAL MEDIA AS PRIMARY, FRAGILE, AND HIDDEN SOURCES

Social media—particularly Facebook, Twitter, and YouTube—also proved to be a hidden source of information for the article. Interviews with editors and conversations on the talk page indicated that social media streams became particularly important sources of information for editors, even if their citations did not reflect this. Social media is another true companion that is often missing from citation lists in breaking news events. Social media sources cited or mentioned on talk pages include the Facebook groups used to organize protests, the Twitter accounts of Egyptians, and the blogs of those active in the protests.

Some editors noted that they used social media sources in order to discover new information related to events and that such awareness catalyzed deeper research into sources more likely to be accepted as reliable on Wikipedia. In a 2014 interview, Ocaasi said,

> Social media inspired research . . . made you look for confirmation for things, but in general, just because something was tweeted, especially if it was just tweeted by an Egyptian protester, that wouldn't be sufficient; we would never cite that. If a journalist who was on the ground in Egypt tweeted something then . . . again, it still exists in this grey area; we would tend to want to wait for a full article to come out to confirm it, but there were definitely . . . there was a bit of blurring of the lines.[21]

Social media sources were deemed useful to editors in some cases, such as when Facebook was used to determine which names were associated with which days of the protests. In one case, editors were confused about the "Day of Anger," the "Friday of Anger," and the "Day of Rage." Lihaas and The Egyptian Liberal confirmed that these are all separate events, with The Egyptian Liberal pointing to the Facebook page from which the "Friday of Anger" name originated.

112.119.91.68: It seems that "Day of Anger" is much more common than "Friday of Anger." That's what Al Jazeera English is using, and dominates in Google hits. Any comment?

But "Day of Rage" (which the BBC is using) gets just about the same number of G-hits as "Day of Anger."

MICHAELZENG7: @The Egyptian Liberal Could you link to that facebook maybe?

LIHAAS: day of anger is a *different* day from yesterdays events. (id guess something that failed)

THE EGYPTIAN LIBERAL: Day of Anger is the 25th . . . Friday of Anger is the 28th . . . and here is the link to the event page on facebook[22]

Despite the use of the Facebook source to verify the titles of protests, the citation is removed shortly afterward. The sections of the article dealing with the role of Facebook and online activism in the protests have only a single link to the April 6 Youth Movement Facebook group mentioned earlier. The citation of the We Are All Khaled Said Facebook group, which catalyzed support for the first protests on January 25, for example, was also removed.

When social media sources are included as citations in the article, they are subsequently removed, not only because they are not considered ideal in terms of policy but also because of problems relating to their archival. Aude recalled how she was following reliable journalists on Twitter but that she preferred to replace Twitter citations with "something more permanent." She told me that they learned who was reliable on Twitter (Al Jazeera journalists, for example) and that "in a pinch you could use something like that, as a source, but when you have the time to go back and fix up the article, it's good to find something that's more permanent."[23]

Social media sources are, therefore, materially fragile because of insecurities about the completeness and permanence of Twitter's archiving systems. Twitter no longer archives all its users' tweets, which means that there is often no permanent URL on Twitter for editors to cite. Other services (such as archive.org) sometimes archive tweets that they believe capture important historic moments, and editors can use free services to archive web pages in order to attach a permanent URL to the sources they cite. The fragility of online sources is also indicated by the fact that, nine years after the article was created, the URLs of a significant proportion of the citations used in the article (12 percent) are no longer available. An additional problem faced by editors was that YouTube videos originally cited in the article appeared to be copyright violations and thus had to be removed.

Although social media sources were highlighted as one of the primary ways in which editors discovered news and information about the events of 2011, bias against these sources, in terms of both policy and technical difficulties, resulted in a significantly steeper rate of removal of social media sources than of traditional media sources. Social media sources acted as the primary channels through which the subjects of the article were able to have their voices heard. Facebook groups that were used to help organize protests, the Twitter accounts of Egyptians, the blogs of those active in the protests, and the footage taken by people during protests were the primary media through which the subjects of the Egyptian revolution of 2011 article could speak.

The iterative removal of these artifacts constituted an iterative exclusion of the voices of the subjects from the article.

WIKIPEDIANS AS WITNESSES

In a talk page exchange on January 28, editors debate the role of protesters in the article. Athinker requests that "unverified comments by protesters" be allowed in the article as a means for protesters to "be able to communicate." Other editors vehemently oppose the request, reiterating the "no original research" principle and affirming the independence of the encyclopedia.

But an interesting comment is made when Wnt suggests the ways in which protesters *could* legitimately become involved in editing the article. They list three "'loopholes' . . . for people involved in the protests to get facts into the article without violating Wikipedia policy": submitting a photo of the events to Wikimedia Commons, creating or joining a partisan website, or writing an article from their perspective for Wikinews. When explaining how protesters might influence the article via Wikimedia Commons, Wnt suggests that

> if you find that Wikipedia is blocked in Egypt, but that you can get around it with an open proxy, you can't just write here that you can do this because it would be original research—but you *can* post photos showing your computer

windows, one blocked, one getting through, and it might make it into the article (I predict debate, though).

Also, since Wikipedia "can report on partisan primary sources that are relatively notable," Wnt asserts that protesters could "put something up on the web that looks like a credible statement from a group of people" so that editors might summarize it as evidence of "one side's opinion."

In his comments, Wnt clearly defines the bounds of "partisan" or subjective viewpoints relating to the events and distinguishes protesters from editors, the latter assumed to simply be objectively summarizing reliable sources rather than attempting to influence the article with their subjective viewpoints. This, remember, is in the context of an article that was created and heavily edited by The Egyptian Liberal, who was clearly involved in the protests while editing the article.

Although Wikipedia's policy of "no original research" means that editors are urged to refrain from contributing their own knowledge to the article, there are actually numerous occasions in which editors bring their own knowledge of the event to bear in making decisions about the article, aside from their selection and positioning of sources as reliable.

One such example is when editors are discussing the Google employee Wael Ghonim, who started the We Are All Khaled Said Facebook group. Editors want to clarify whether Ghonim is still the administrator of the Facebook group. The Egyptian Liberal, in Egypt at the time and with personal connections to protesters and activists on the ground, is able to verify Ghonim's status as administrator.

"I just spoke to Wael and no, he is still the admin of the page," he writes on the talk page on February 7. No one opposes this assertion, and, apparently, there is no need to cite The Egyptian Liberal as the source of the fact's confirmation, even though he is critical to its presence in the article.[24]

THE MANY COMPANIONS TO WIKIPEDIA'S FACTS

Considering Wikipedia's sources—both those that are clearly attributed and those that remain hidden—is vital to understanding how truth on Wikipedia is established and what the true sources of its shaping are. Following editors' practices in cocreating the article, I learned how crucial those practices are in determining the underlying narrative of the article. In addition to an article's cited sources, facts' traveling companions include the platforms that surface articles to be summarized in order to produce those very facts. They include the hidden sources that are used to uncover information: the experts and witnesses that are hidden because they are invalid sources according to Wikipedia policy.

Understanding Wikipedia's true companions enables us to recognize what sources inform the particular direction that the narrative takes. The choice of sources is critical for deciding whose narrative the article tends to be more aligned toward. It also demonstrates a potential weakness in Wikipedia's procedures for determining the truth of the event.

It appears to Wikipedians, and often to readers, that editors play a passive role of objectively summarizing sources of only the best quality as events unfold over time. In fact, Wikipedians' sourcing practice indicates how critical Wikipedians and their editing are in shaping the article. Editors decide which sources are considered "reliable," based on the market for sources at the time they require them. Editors confirm some reports and deny others based on their embodied experiences as witnesses to events. And editors use platforms that influence their discovery and highlighting of some information rather than other information, and they make selections from chosen sources to emphasize some features and actors in the narrative rather than others.

* * *

As protests enter their third week, facts in the Egyptian protests article are traveling well, helped along by multiple companions. The nationwide protest itself continues unabated, and the question on everyone's mind now is whether the protesters will succeed in their demands. Will President Hosni Mubarak resign? Will the Egyptian government accept the definition of events by protesters? In order for this to happen, we need a speech act by Mubarak or his representatives that effectively declares defeat, and we need mediated representations to accept this and represent it as the cathartic end to the disruption and upheaval. This is not inevitable. Protests could continue on a rolling boil.

What will happen next requires effort from multiple forces working to reinforce the core narrative: that the people of Egypt want Mubarak out, that the people are this story's victims, and that it is Hosni Mubarak that is the root of Egypt's problems.

5

SURGE

Until now, Wikipedia and most major news outlets have classified events in Egypt as "major protests." Although some have tried to change their classification to "revolution," they have failed and their edits have been reverted. In order for facts under such global attention to be reclassified, official utterances need to be spoken on the ground (in this case, the words "I resign"), and a myriad of representative forces need to work together in unison to achieve the collective renaming. This renaming will not be without a fight: crowds descend on knowledge platforms like Wikipedia in order to write history as it happens, even if those actions are too early by Wikipedia's encyclopedic standards. Figure 5.1 illustrates events on Wikipedia as they are described in this chapter.

EGYPT: FEBRUARY 10 AND 11, 2011

By the second week of February, the protesters' anger and frustration have reached an all-time high. Of all the protesters' demands, it is the call for President Hosni Mubarak to resign that is the most vehement. Hundreds of protesters have been killed by security forces, and Mubarak has appeared ruthless and out of touch during public appearances. The man who has ruled Egypt for thirty years is collectively recognized as the

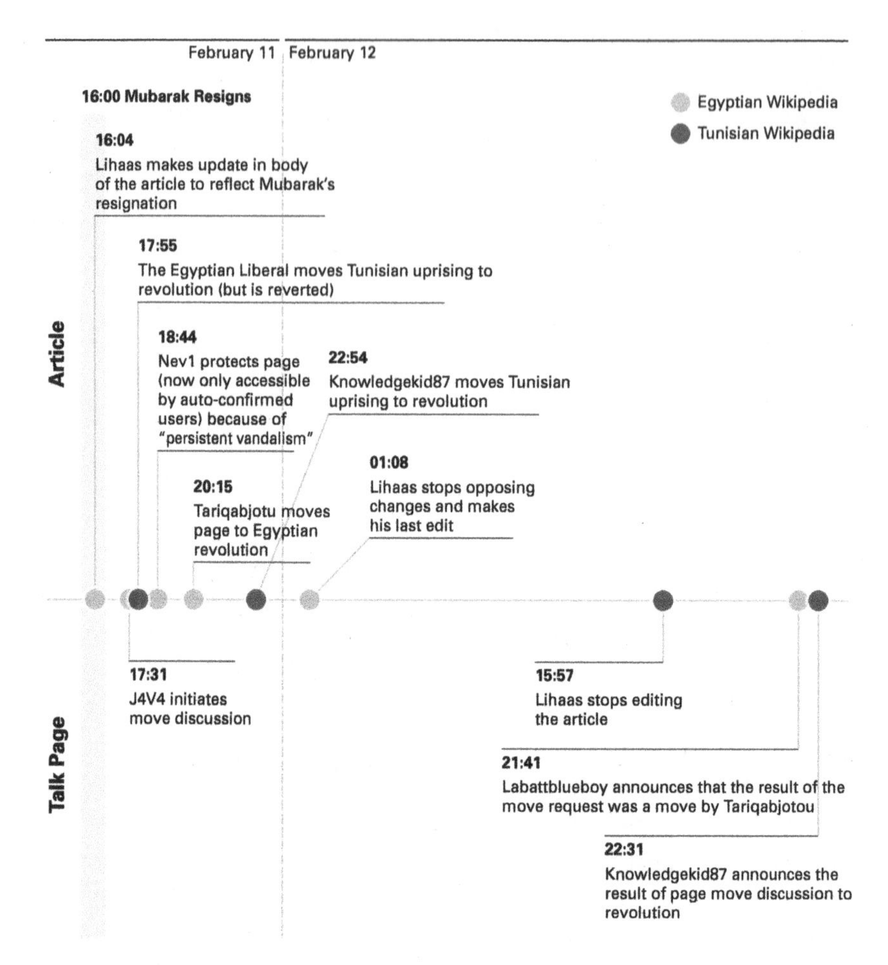

5.1 Timeline of significant changes to English Wikipedia 48 hours after Hosni Mubarak's resignation on February 11, 2011

source of its problems. In order for the country to enter a new era, its old guard will need to depart willingly or be driven from office.

Opposition figures and the government have been meeting to discuss a resolution to the crisis, but those talks are on the brink of collapse. The world is watching to see what the Egyptian military will do in the face of the public disorder. On February 10, General Hassan al-Roueini, the military commander of Cairo, tells protesters, "All your demands will be met today." The atmosphere in the streets changes—protesters in Tahrir Square

are reported to be joyful and excited in expectation of Mubarak's resignation. But the moment is also steeped in trepidation. Many are concerned that behind the scenes the military might have seized control and that this will usher in a new authoritarian regime. Confusion is fueled by contradictory reports from media sources around the world that either Vice President Omar Suleiman or commander in chief of the Egyptian Armed Forces Mohamed Tantawi will take over from Mubarak.

It is 8:00 p.m. local time. Mubarak is due to deliver a public address via state television. At 8:46 p.m. he begins to deliver a long, rambling speech about his role as the unyielding father of the nation. In a weak attempt to appease protesters, Mubarak announces that he is delegating most of his powers to the vice president and that he will not contest the next presidential election, due to take place later in the year. He concludes that he will stay in his post and die on Egyptian soil.

The speech creates uncertainty and confusion among the international press. A story from the Associated Press is headlined "Egypt's Mubarak Transfers Power to Vice President." But the *New York Times* reports that "Mubarak refuses to step down." According to Jack Shenkar, a *Guardian* journalist in Tahrir Square at the time, "When it became clear that Mubarak intended to stay on until September, the square shook with fury."[1] The protesters erupt in anger, crying, waving their shoes in the air, and chanting "Leave! Leave! Leave!"

The next day, February 11, an infuriated public takes to the streets. On the morning of the largest protest to date, the military announces that they support a gradual transition to democracy in the country but fail to denounce either Mubarak or Suleiman as being part of that transition. They state that they will guarantee changes to the constitution, as well as free and fair elections, but they will only lift the thirty-year-old state of emergency (a key demand from protesters) "as soon as current circumstances end."

By midday, there are reports of protests spreading across Cairo. After Friday prayers, protesters fan out to the presidential palace and other key symbols of the authoritarian regime, in a new push to force Mubarak to resign. As the protesters amass around the palace, Mubarak and his family are seen leaving by helicopter. Another enraged crowd marches on the state television building, viewed as a pro-Mubarak bastion that has supported Mubarak and dismissed the protests. The crowd swarms to the foot of the building, beating drums and chanting.

In the afternoon, there are reports that a statement from the presidency is due "soon." At 6:00 p.m., Omar Suleiman reads a short speech over state television. In an address lasting just thirty seconds, Suleiman announces that Hosni Mubarak has "decided to give up his position as President of the Republic and instructed the supreme council of the armed forces to manage the affairs of the country."

Crowds outside the state television station are stunned. According to *Guardian* correspondent Chris McGreal, who was outside the station when the announcement was made,

> There was a pause. Then a ripple went through the crowd and they went wild. Some fell onto their knees praying, people were weeping instantly. They were hugging each other, chanting in unison, "Mubarak's gone," words to that effect. There was joy, euphoria, call it what you want. I think people couldn't quite grasp that this revolution that they'd led (for) eighteen days had finally delivered.[2]

Mohamed ElBaradei, the leader of the opposition movement, tells international media, "This is the greatest day of my life. The country has been liberated after decades of repression." He says that he expects a "beautiful" transition of power.[3]

Celebrations reverberate around the world. Moments after the announcement, fireworks light up the sky over Beirut. In Tunisia, people shout with joy and honk their horns when they hear the news. The governments of Jordan, Iraq, and Sudan send their blessings. Two hours after the announcement, US president Barack Obama's response is carried live over Egyptian state television. He congratulates the Egyptian people for their nonviolent actions to bring about democracy in the country: "Tahrir means liberation, and it is a word that speaks to something in our souls that cries out for freedom—and will forever more remind us of the Egyptian people."[4]

EUPHORIA

Within hours of the announcement, news organizations, journalists, and political authorities move from classifying events as "protests" to referring to them as a "revolution." This is a key moment in the story of the event.

Reclassification requires a myriad of representative forces working in unison in order to achieve the collective renaming. Those forces, including the media and Wikipedia, play a critical role in the transformative nature of these moments. The rites and symbols that serve as powerful agents of change during such events are re-presented by those telling the story of events, but *new* symbols—in the form of categories, myths, and legends—are also generated by mediated forms. That process, however, does not happen without a struggle at individual sites of representation. It is to this struggle on Wikipedia that we now turn.

The battle to classify events in Egypt has been ongoing on Wikipedia since the first days of the protests. As we saw in the last chapter, proposals were made at an early stage to change the page title from Egyptian "protests" to "uprising," with some editors even proposing the term "revolution," on the basis that the scale of the protests warranted the term. One editor attempted to change the article title to "2011 Egyptian Revolution" on the second and third days of the protests, but the edits were reverted on both occasions. Until the moment of Mubarak's resignation, editors failed to gain consensus on the most accurate term for the events.

In the minutes and hours after Mubarak's resignation, a new crowd of editors surges into the "2011 Egyptian protests" namespace on Wikipedia. The ultimate goal of this crowd is to participate in the writing of history.

Where are the key sites of struggle on Wikipedia in which this battle for classification takes place? The most important classification battle is, first, to change the article title from "protests" to "revolution," using the process of what is known as a page move. Technically, a page move requires the editor to select an option from a drop-down menu in the navigation bar of an edit window in order to begin the process. Not everyone knows how to do this, and so page moves tend to be associated with experienced editors.

The second is to change the key facts summarizing events in the infobox and lead paragraph of the article, as well as its categories. Such battles are conducted on two fronts: in the article itself, where editors must make changes that will endure and not be reverted, and on the article's talk page, where editors must justify their actions and debate with others who are arguing against such changes.

In the pages that follow, I zoom in on the article and talk page—the inner workings of Wikipedia—in order to describe how the decision to change the classification of the article from "protests" to "revolution" plays out. Here we will move between the article space, in which coded actions are taking place to change the way in which events are represented, and the talk page of the article, in which those changes are being discussed. There are many policies and procedures that could stand in the way of making this change so soon after the announcement. How, then, is this victory achieved on Wikipedia? Who leads it? What logics and tactics determine such decisions?

BATTLE FOR CONTROL OF THE NARRATIVE

The editor Lihaas becomes crucial in this stage of the article's development.

At the time of writing, Lihaas is blocked on English Wikipedia for abusing multiple accounts or "sockpuppeting." A sockpuppet is an online identity created for the purposes of deception. Editors may create multiple user profiles on Wikipedia and use them to swell votes or opinions along a particular line of argument. Lihaas has appealed the block, arguing that it is a case of "mistaken identity." He describes himself on his user page as suffering from PTSD and has written, "The sanity of this user is disputed."

Lihaas started editing in 2008 and has created scores of articles. He has a number of barnstars (Wikipedia awards) on his page, including that he is ranked among the top Wikipedia editors for article creation. He has edited hundreds of articles relating to global politics and has done some paid editing for companies. Lihaas is transparent about his political views on his user page. He "supports the democratic movement in Bahrain," is "opposed to the House of Saud," and is "a Confederate citizen." He states, "Let's also not forget the Roma and Slavs that were killed, amongst others, in the Holocaust!"

When Mubarak's resignation is announced at just after 6:00 p.m. on February 11, Lihaas is working intensively on the article and leading discussions on the talk page. At 6:04 p.m., he hastily makes the historic change to the article by adding a single line to the body. The haste with which this was added is visible in the typos here: "Vice Presidenty Oman Suleiman announced that the Presidency has been vacated and the army council would run the country."

Lihaas adds *"HES GONE! BRWEAKIGN NEWS!!!!"* to the edit summary, visible on the history tab of the article.

THE FIRST FRONT: CHANGING THE ARTICLE TITLE

Immediately after the announcement of Mubarak's resignation, the crowd editing the article swells with newcomers. The makeup of both the editors and the readers of the article changes at this pivotal moment. In the same way that the day of Mubarak's resignation saw the highest numbers of protesters and viewers of media coverage of events in Egypt, on Wikipedia there is a significant increase in the numbers of editors and readers of the article. The result is an important shift in the dynamics of the cohort working on the article that propels the most significant changes to the meaning of events that it represents.

In the hour after Mubarak's resignation, the number of users accessing the page triples from about 4,000 to 12,500 users—by the end of the day, 125,000 users have accessed the page. The number of editors also swells in that hour. Many are anonymous users from the United States, UK, Canada, the Netherlands, Portugal, and Singapore, and the majority of these editors are new to the article, overwhelming those who have been editing it consistently from the beginning.

Within minutes, multiple editors attempt to change key facts that reclassify the article from "protests" to "revolution." They are continually reverted. This edit war lasts about seven and a half hours as three experienced Wikipedia editors (notably Lihaas but also Ocaasi and, initially, Muboshgu) struggle to hold back the flood of editors attempting to make these significant changes to the article before consensus is reached. Two hours after the resignation is announced, an administrator protects the article by preventing anonymous users from editing, but this doesn't stop the continual edits by registered users in their attempt to alter the core classification of the article.

The newcomers employ a number of tactics to try to alter the article's classification. These include both direct and covert maneuvers at key locations in the article: the page name, the infobox summaries, the first line of the article, and the category section.

In direct classification action, editors attempt to change the title of the page, the title of the infobox, and the definition in the first line from "protests" to "revolution." These are strategic locations for classification because of their summarizing function (many readers will read only the summaries of articles in the first paragraph and the visual infobox) and because it is these locations that automated processes target when extracting information for presentation on other sites.

Editors also attempt more covert actions by defining the current date as the end date of the phenomenon, for example. The date field in the infobox is changed from "25 January 2011–ongoing" to "25 January 2011–11 February 2011."

The tense in the first line of the article is changed from present to past tense: from "The Egyptian protests of 2011 are a series of street demonstrations" to "The Egyptian protests of 2011 were a series of street demonstrations."

By changing the tense of this critical fact in the article, editors are attempting to signal the end of the event, thereby classifying Suleiman's performative utterance of Mubarak's resignation as conclusive.

Classification is also attempted through other covert routes—by adding "revolution" to the "characteristics" field of the infobox and by adding the category "21st Century revolutions" to the end of the article. In doing so, editors attempt to link events in Egypt to other events already stably defined as revolutions.

In response, more experienced editors defend the article against edits that would change the fundamental classification of events so soon after the speech was made. Ocaasi reverts edits to classify the article but stops after a few hours. Muboshgu initially reverts edits but, a few hours later, joins the group attempting to change the article's classification to revolution. Lihaas, on the other hand, continues to revert edits to the classification of the article for the next five hours. In one edit summary, he implores that "the event is not over in 4 (hours)!"

In addition to directly reverting edits to the classification of the article as a revolution, Lihaas also attempts more indirect strategies, such as destabilizing the entire article by warning readers about its current volatility, and by attempting to communicate correct procedure with editors whom he sees as making preemptive changes. In one attempt, Lihaas adds a warning tag to the head of the page—"The neutrality of this article is disputed"—and urges editors to go to the talk page for discussion. In another, he adds a "dubious" tag to the date of events when it is clear that his efforts to directly revert edits are not working. Lihaas constantly tries to coordinate the actions of editors in the article by adding hidden notes (visible only to editors rather than readers) requesting that editors not change the infobox title until consensus has been reached.

An hour and a half after Mubarak's resignation is announced, a discussion is initiated on the talk page in which editors are asked to weigh in on whether the title of the article should be changed to "revolution." A page move of this significance requires consensus from editors on the talk page of the article, according to Wikipedia policy.[5] The final decision on the name change is announced on the talk page a day later, on the evening of February 12.

But the page is moved about three hours after the discussion was initiated—that is, long before the decision to move the page is announced. Surprisingly, no editor reverts this move, despite its being performed before the final decision on the survey is announced.

THE SECOND FRONT: DISCUSSIONS ON THE TALK PAGE

The Wikipedia editor J4V4 initiates the survey on the talk page in which editors are asked to debate the possibility of changing the article name to "revolution." J4V4 has been editing for about two years before this but in their second year faced charges of vandalism, sockpuppeting, and trolling. Their "final warning" (for alleged trolling) was received the month before the events in Egypt. The only contribution they make to this article is the move request on the talk page. J4V4 calls for opinions, writing, "Now that Mubarak has been forced out of power, many major news outlets are referring to it as a revolution."

In order to rename the target title (or to "move" the page to a new home) for potentially contentious subjects, Wikipedia policy[6] indicates that a discussion needs to happen in order for editors to reach consensus on the article title before making the change. This policy provides guidelines on who is able to contribute to the discussion (anyone) and make the final decision on the name change (an "uninvolved editor," ideally an administrator). It also provides guidance about the format of the discussion, as well as the process that should be followed, both of which reflect more general principles around consensus on Wikipedia.

When making arguments in favor of or against the proposed name change, policy dictates that editors disclose whether they have a vested interest in the article. They are also urged to read the article, look at its history, and read earlier comments and recommendations before making an argument to either support or oppose the name change. Editors should be familiar with the policy and norms around article titling (in general, as well as specific to events, and breaking news events in particular) and should make arguments that explain how the proposed title meets or violates policy.

The focus of the policy is on encouraging editors to make rational arguments framed in terms of Wikipedia editing principles. An oft-quoted phrase from the policy is that the discussion "is not a vote." In other words, editors shouldn't merely state their preferences and/or opinions about whether the change should or shouldn't occur, but rather should support their positions with reference to evidence and policy. The editor closing the discussion should, in turn, make a final decision by evaluating arguments. Precedence should be given to arguments that refer to relevant Wikipedia rules and norms.

The policy also states that if there are objections to the proposed move with "no clear indication from policy and conventions" on what to do about the change, then this "normally" means that no change happens. If editors believe that the move was closed unreasonably, then they may request a review of the move. They may also use Wikipedia's dispute resolution process to sanction editors who "persist" with "disruptive behavior."

The format of the discussion is framed interchangeably using the terms "discussion" and "survey." Editors are asked to begin their responses with the word "support" or "oppose," followed by their reasons, and to sign their responses. Other editors may comment on those responses using indented lines.

Forty-seven editors participate in the survey—forty-one support a change to "revolution" and six are opposed. Only about a quarter of those supporting the move have edited the article, and four have never edited Wikipedia before. Only four have made more than five edits on the article.

An examination of the discussion reflects that a process very different from the ideal specified in the policy has been followed. The arguments generally lack reference to specific policies relating to name changes, in contrast to the guidelines in name change policy.

In his study of the 2005 London bombings, Christian Pentzold characterizes arguments in favor of and against the labeling of events as "terrorist" acts according to six types of argumentation.[7] In the discussion we are focusing on, arguments in favor of the change include what Pentzold terms "the definition argument." "[It] is a true revolution" is a common refrain. Others use Pentzold's "common sense argument," with one editor writing that it is "ludicrous that [the page hasn't] yet been renamed." About a third of the supporters justify their opinions by arguing that authorities are now representing events as a "revolution," which means that Wikipedia should follow suit.

Pentzold has a category for "the reasonable consensus of the majority argument," which he defines with examples relating to consensus of the media and government and the presumed consensus among academics for particular terms. However, the arguments put forward in the talk page survey relating to consensus among reliable sources aren't offered as evidence of majority consensus, but rather as evidence of particular authorities' perspectives. This might be called an "authoritative sources argument" and consists of utterances that describe which authorities are defining events as a revolution as evidence of its conclusiveness. These statements are performative because in making their utterances, they change the reality of that which they are describing, adding to the perceived authority and reliability of the sources they use as evidence.

Those authorities are generally vaguely identified as "the media," but there is also reference to Obama's recognition of events as a revolution (even though Obama did not, in fact, refer to events as revolutionary). One editor even refers to Wikipedia's own definition of "revolution." Those referring to "the media" generally provide qualitative judgments about quantities (for example, "every" media outlet or "almost all" are referring to events as a revolution) without specifying which media they are referring to. The Egyptian Liberal links to a Google Trends graph as evidence of the rise in usage of the term.

Others refer generally to the quality of the sources (for example, "most major media" are saying revolution), without specifying how they are evaluating the term "major." Only four editors refer to specific media outlets (including CNN, the *Washington Post,* and Al Jazeera). Silver seren adds an appendix to the survey that provides a list of twelve "reliable sources" using the term (nine of which are US based and one from Egypt [*Al-Ahram*]) but does not participate according to the "support" or "oppose" format.

Those opposing the motion refer to Wikipedia's policies on original research and urge a more measured decision-making process. Half of the opposers point out that the change will break Wikipedia's "No Original Research" rule, which forbids the inclusion of facts "for which no reliable, published sources exist" or that "imply a conclusion not stated by the sources." Whereas those arguing for the change write that it is important that Wikipedia not fall "behind the curve" in its representation of events, those opposing it urge editors to wait and see, arguing that "as editors we are supposed to be 'behind the curve'" (Midlakewinter) and that they should not make such a significant change during "the heat of the moment" (Lihaas).

Guerilla tries to oppose some of those contributing to the poll by commenting on the votes of three supporters that either haven't contributed to the article or are sockpuppets. The implication by Guerilla is either that editors have been canvased simply to vote on the article rather than to contribute meaningfully or they have multiplied their votes by using alternative user profiles.

Many of the editors of the Egyptian protests article have also been working on articles relating to other events taking place in the region. Over at the article about events in Tunisia, which resulted in the overthrow of then-president Ben Ali the previous month, there had been similar discussions about the renaming of the article—with many of the same editors involved. In earlier talk page discussions about the title of the Egyptian protests article, some editors argued that events in Egypt could hardly be named as a "revolution" when the article about its neighbor Tunisia was still represented as "protests."

A discussion about renaming the Tunisian uprising article had been ongoing on the talk page of that article since February 2, but no editor tried to change the name of the article to "revolution." Multiple editors used the number of Google hits for Tunisian revolution versus Tunisian uprising as a basis for their support. Lihaas opposed the change, at one stage arguing, "Wikipedia is not based on *google hits* we [don't] cater to public opinion. Otherwise [it] would be 'googlepedia' and it [wouldn't] be reliable." He asked for evidence from reliable sources and concluded that "consensus is not built by vote [counting]."[8]

There were no moves to conclude the discussion on the Tunisian page, or to rename the article, until the day of Mubarak's resignation, February 11. About two hours after the announcement is made, The Egyptian Liberal tries to move the Tunisian article from "2010–2011 Tunisian Uprising" to "2010–2011 Tunisian Revolution." His edits are reverted.

About two hours later, over at the Egyptian protests article, the title of the article is changed from "protests" to "revolution" before the discussion about the change is concluded on the talk page. This historic change is made by Tariqabjotu,[9] an experienced Wikipedian who declares on his user page that he started editing in 2005, that he designed the current events portal, and that he became an administrator in 2006. He summarizes the edit[10] by explaining that he has "moved 2011 Egyptian protests to Egyptian revolution of 2011" and refers editors to the talk page where he declares that there is "overwhelming consensus already" and that the "prominence necessitates decision," thereby applying Pentzold's "reasonable consensus of the majority argument."

Two editors, Lihaas and Guerilla, vehemently oppose the process by which the decision is being made on the talk page and are upset that the move occurs while discussion is still taking place, just hours after the proposal was put forward. Lihaas argues that the move constitutes a "unilateral and unexplained change while discussion is ongoing" and that it prevents editors in other time zones from participating in the discussion. Lihaas also comments on one supporting editor's position that "consensus is not determined over 3 hours heated with breaking news." But Tariqabjotu retorts, "There is no doubt now that there is consensus that revolution should be in the title" and that "the 'revolution' discussion has been going on for a long time."

Over at the Tunisian protests article, Knowledgekid87 then successfully moves the Tunisian page to "revolution" without opposition. About eight hours after editing the article to reflect Mubarak's resignation, Lihaas seems to give up on efforts to police revolutionary edits to the page. He does not revert an edit to the infobox title made a few hours later, and he makes a final edit of the article shortly after that. Lihaas will offer only one more edit of the article, three years later.

A day after the name change survey is initiated, an announcement confirming the name change is made. There are no formal objections to the process made outside of the talk page of the article.

"DON'T DENY HISTORY!"

In July 2018, Ocaasi and I had an email conversation about the ways in which the decision to change the article's title was made. I was confused about the article being renamed long before the discussion on the talk page was concluded, and that not a single editor had opposed the move, despite it going against policy. It seemed a failure to me. Something had gone wrong.

Ocaasi acknowledged that the page move may have been improper according to policy, but he had a number of reasons to explain why it wasn't reverted. He admitted that discussion closures are unpredictable because they have no set timeline and "anyone can close them at any time." He argued, though, that Wikipedia had still been following what reliable sources were saying about events, and therefore the move was justifiable.

More importantly, though, Ocaasi wrote about the ways in which the reclassification of events as a revolution reflected how he and the other editors surrendered to the momentousness of the occasion and that any effort to resist changes to the article's title would have been swimming against a tide of editors, one of whom declared that Wikipedia shouldn't "deny history."

"There were a continuing influx of support votes outweighing oppose votes, so reverting would have been going against the 'trend' in the discussion," he wrote. According to Ocaasi, the announcement was "historic and globally momentous" and the editors "were enthralled and excited by real world events and more concerned with the spirit than the letter of page move policy at that time."

I was so exhilarated and exhausted by this point that the title change was the least of my thoughts. I was thinking of the people in Tahrir and how they had triumphed and my hopes for what they could bring to the aftermath of the revolution, hopefully a new beginning.

In February 2011, Wikipedia's reclassification of events in Egypt—from protests to revolution—is achieved through the material actions of a large, distributed crowd. Those actions, like the dismantling of monuments and the public buildings in Cairo, are directed toward strategic points in the article's infrastructure and in neighboring articles that become strategic in relation to the reclassification.

Within the article, skirmishes occur in the article title, infobox statements, categories, and opening statements. The revolutionary title change requires an equally historic change to a neighboring article, that of the Tunisian protests. This is because Wikipedians are aware that their classification of events as revolutionary, as a result of the president's resignation, embodies a definition of revolution that then should logically be extended to events in Tunisia, which have previously not been accorded that status.

Although Wikipedia might have followed sources in changing the name of events in Egypt from "protest" to "revolution" (however rapidly), Wikipedia's classification of events in Tunisia as revolutionary positions it much more as a precursor. In this way, we see how the ripple effect of events in the Arab Spring is materially manifested by the mirroring of classification actions. Wikipedia has an extraordinary impact in leading efforts to connect events to one another, and therefore to narrate their rationale and effects.

Wikipedia classifies events in Egypt as a revolution before those of Tunisia, even though the latter's leader vacated weeks before Mubarak. Egypt perhaps has many more forces with an incentive to propel events toward revolution than does Tunisia, as evidenced by the large numbers in the United States who tune in to watch events in Egypt. Tunisian protesters benefit from the attention directed toward Egypt and the forces behind the revolutionary narrative, just as Egyptian protesters benefit from the revolutionary story initiated by their neighbors weeks earlier.

Such are the features of editorial decisions made during moments of collective effervescence,[11] a kind of delirium described by French sociologist Émile Durkheim that is experienced by crowds of people during ritualized assemblies and commemorations. In these moments, Wikipedia mirrors the intense emotion, passion, and energy that occurred in one of the event's epicenters in Tahrir Square. In this moment, it is a new, relatively inexperienced crowd that displaces the smaller group of experienced editors who were previously in control of the article.

The sentiment that guides this crowd is characterized by a fetishization of the collective rather than a reasoned attempt to reach consensus. It is the material force in numbers that ultimately guarantees success in changing the article title before the deliberative exercise on the talk page has been concluded. Although Wikipedia urges editors to write in the neutral point of view and to reach consensus on controversial issues through rational dialogue, Wikipedia is not outside of the sphere of collective effervescence, and so decisions like these are made by the force of the crowd rather than according to the principles of deliberation.

Indeed, what we see happening in the hours after Mubarak's resignation—the struggle on Wikipedia to reclassify events as revolutionary—is an echo of the same dynamics that characterized the final days of protests.

The logics that drive the crowd in Cairo are dominated by a reverence for the collective rather than any careful, deliberative, or reasoned approach. So, too, on Wikipedia, where the logics that abound during the decision-making process are far from consistent with Wikipedia's ideal notion of rational decision-making driven by the contribution of reasoned arguments and evidence toward the achievement of consensus. Many of those who are able to influence the classification are part of the collective and under the influence of the surge in emotion that accompanies events in Egypt.

The crowd that flows into the article in this historic moment is relatively inexperienced, and so they require more experienced editors to make lasting changes at the most strategic points in the article. This work involves software tactics that require what Stuart Geiger and I have called "trace literacy"—the background, organizational knowledge of the ways in which information flows across the encyclopedia, and the grammars required to make changes that hold.[12] Software tactics that change the way in which a phenomenon is encoded, and represented at scale, are critical to successful activism in the representation of events on Wikipedia. The most fundamental change to the article—the front in the battle to control the meaning of events—is at the canonical page name.

As we have seen, Tariqabjotu makes this change just over two hours after Mubarak's resignation was announced, and long before the discussion about the change is concluded on the talk page. His action and explanation at this particular moment in time are successful because of his performative abilities. Not only does he know how to perform a page move technically, but he also knows how to justify his actions. Tariqabjotu declares there is already "overwhelming consensus," adding a sense of urgency because of the "prominence" of the article.

Editors who wish to withhold such changes until deliberative decision-making is concluded must fight what they see as the premature classification of the article on at least two fronts: both at the article itself, where activist editors are attempting to change the material classification of the event in strategic locations, and at the talk page discussion. These editors remove the last vestiges of the old order from the page through its replacement with new categories.

In this way, the crowd logic practiced here overwhelms the deliberative process. Crowd logic is necessarily populist—its power lies in gesturing toward what "everyone" believes is "obviously" true, rather than the quality of arguments or evidence, or the expertise and experience of particular sources. In the absence of rigorous methods for evaluating consensus among reliable sources within the conditions of rapid editing, there is no other option than to submit to those declaring that there is consensus according to heuristics relating to popularity and quantity. The language used to argue for the name change includes declarative statements: that it is "obviously" a revolution, and that "the media" and critical authorities are calling it a revolution.

No editor reverts Tariqabjotu's change, and the lack of opposition in editing means that, according to Wikipedia's standards, there is consensus. At this critical point, some of the editors who have been involved in the discussion from the beginning now step back. According to Lihaas, others are not involved because they are working in a different time zone. In this case, opposing editors clearly give up their efforts to withstand the surge of sentiment because it becomes clear that there aren't enough editors to oppose them or even the right tools or discourses to help stem the tide.

If we look at the talk page, we could say that consensus is not reached and that this is a failure of Wikipedia's decision-making process. But this ignores the fact that the default approach to consensus building on Wikipedia is assumed to take place through editing rather than discussion. According to the policy on consensus, "Any edit that is not disputed or reverted by another editor can be assumed to have consensus." There are, of course, multiple reasons why the conclusion of opposing edits does not indicate agreement. But the policy doesn't require that all editors agree with the decision, nor does it stipulate that any discussion must continue for a period of time that guarantees the greatest participation (particularly among editors who are geographically dispersed).

Further, piecing together the reasons why a particular decision was made (the name change, for example) is complex, and many pieces are often missing. Where do we look for the discussion that resulted in the decision? Certainly not to the talk page, where the decision to rename the page came before the debate was concluded. Piecing together the steps toward renaming requires piecing together multiple conversations and actions across the target article as well as related articles (the Tunisian revolution article, for example). Rather than representing a failure of Wikipedia's decision-making process, this example reflects the weaknesses of Wikipedia's approach to deliberation.

Many have lauded Wikipedia's communitarian approach to deliberation. Comparing Wikipedia with commercial platforms like Google and Facebook, Kate Crawford and Tarleton Gillespie[13] argue that Wikipedia's discussion pages offer thicker communication opportunities where "the quality of content is openly debated and the decisions to keep or remove content on that basis are visible and preserved over time." But rather than a visible log of deliberation toward decisions, we see here two parallel processes for decision-making that contradict one another but where action ultimately trumps discussion.

The prominence of the article (the fact that the world is watching), and the necessity of Wikipedia being "up to date," overcomes Wikipedia's consensus-building ideal, which relies on rational, considered, and potentially lengthy discussions involving all editors. This is because the process they are relying on does not suit the timing and dynamics of the global media event that the Egyptian revolution represents.

Contrasting decision-making in the ideal and the ways in which it works in practice in breaking news articles reflects a tension between two goals of Wikipedia: retaining a neutral point of view and reflecting current information. The process of changing the name of the article, the classification of events, and the fundamental meaning of what is happening in Egypt represent how decision-making structures designed for representing relatively stable, consensual knowledge come up against the volatility and uncertainty that characterize the representation of political events in the current media environment.

STRUGGLE IN THE SQUARE, STRUGGLE IN THE NAMESPACE

Defining an event according to a particular classification is a political struggle that accompanies the very material realities of protest, war, and attack. It is a struggle that is, by definition, mediated—wrapped up in the representations of the event from the moment the first crowds arrive in the square, the first shots are fired, and the first explosions are heard. Over time, that struggle lessens as consensus is reached on the meaning of an event. But such meanings are still subject to struggle over longer periods of time—when anniversaries of the event are celebrated, for example—because they are seen in the context of new realities, new power dynamics between the groups affected.

While Wikipedia re-presents symbols and concepts from authoritative accounts, it also does important work to generate the fundamental categories that frame the historical account through strategic classification. This isn't just any classification. It is an act that will reverberate through other important representative accounts (as we will see starkly in the next chapter). In this act of renaming, Wikipedia editors are able to participate in the claim of victory, to determine the encyclopedic classification of events, and thus to (literally) make history—to construct it using the very terms in which events will be framed and remembered.

Wikipedia becomes another Tahrir Square—a place dominated by crowd logics in which crowds must collectively stabilize their narrative and classification of events. The only difference is that the process is taking place on the internet, using data. Wikipedia serves as yet another space in which symbolic rites are both enacted and generated, drawing from signs and symbols that are being represented by digitally mediated forms.

Rather than a space in which rational decision-making occurs according to consensus, Wikipedia mirrors many of the features of collective effervescence. An almost religious euphoria resounds across the world in the hours after Mubarak's resignation. Collective effervescence stands in opposition to reasoned dialogue guided by deliberation. The term is used to characterize moments of intense passion when crowds gather together to enact and generate rites and symbols, particularly in relation to religious gatherings. For Durkheim, the outcome of collective effervescence was to strengthen—indeed, make sacred—the collectivity itself. Although he was largely studying religious rituals, he showed that rituals also take place in secular life. Protests are a modern form of ritual in which the collective becomes sacred.[14]

In Egypt, we see the protest ritual performed continually through the preceding weeks, and a number of key symbols generated and enacted during those protests: the symbol of the martyr as a reminder of the importance of the struggle; the physical tearing down of buildings, like the television station that was seen as representing the interests of Mubarak at the expense of protesters; protesters holding up shoes in response to Mubarak's speech on February 10, in which he did not conclusively resign, indicating their contempt for him.

In this moment, the euphoria in celebration of the collective against the will of the dictator is at its peak. This juncture is signified by the process of reclassification, where those representing events name them as a "revolution," replacing "protests" or "uprising." According to Wagner-Pacifici, the process of classifying, serializing, genealogizing, or analogizing helps "resolve the unease of the rupture's incoherence."[15] Moments of collective effervescence are, by their nature, temporary and must be resolved. These rites and symbols must be replicated in order to turn a rupture into a transformative event. Such a transformation is determined by a collective meaning-making process in which the inexplicable and formless are made explicable and given a form.[16] This is achieved not through reasoned dialogue and rational consensus building but through the shared participation in passionate rituals.

The moment of celebration by crowds and leaders following Mubarak's resignation is represented across television news and major Western newspapers as a conclusive moment, a turning point, the culmination of collective efforts, a landmark event, milestone, watershed. What these terms share is their marking of an edge or a boundary. Like an ancient milestone marking the distance in miles from a given point, symbolic milestones enable us to locate ourselves in time and space. The reclassification of events serves as a way of establishing sightlines, horizons, and orientations—it enables us to emerge from the earlier disruption. Out of chaos and confusion come stability and relief. And so it makes sense that we ignore the inherent uncertainty and ambiguity that come with any turning point, blank page, or movement toward radical change.

These features include the arrival of an even larger crowd of newcomers who drive the narrative to a collective conclusion, the overwhelming emotion that displaces what is usually recognized as the ideal conditions of rational debate, a turn to similar voices as authoritative in supporting the popular classification of events, and the use of declarative language in support of decisions. Unique to Wikipedia are the types of strategies required to enable classifications to take hold. The most powerful representative forces in this moment are those who can take coded action in addition to discursive action (that is, offering the best argument using written text), but both are necessary in order to present the appearance of collective action.

Tahrir Square and Wikipedia are two sites of struggle in which the battle to classify events in Egypt plays out. Both are sites of concentrated action and focus in determining the future of events at the pivotal moment surrounding Mubarak's resignation. The ritual actions taking place within these spaces produce both form and explanation of the inexplicable and formless state that characterizes moments of social upheaval. Far from the encyclopedic space being one of emotionally detached deliberation in which decisions are made rationally, it is, rather, a mirror of the emotional intensity and nonrationality that characterize Tahrir Square. In fact, some of those who are involved and enacting struggle tactics can be found in both spaces.

How, then, do we understand the decision-making that resulted in the name change on Wikipedia happening before the discussion had been concluded on the talk page? Is this merely a mindless action by an unthinking mob? A reflection of how decision-making regularly occurs on Wikipedia?

The first point to make is that, although the crowd making the change is certainly emotional and not enacting rational procedures preferred by policy, they are not mindless. Discussing moments of collective effervescence, Tim Olaveson[17] notes that although the outcome of collective delirium is uncertain, the people participating in the ritual are not deluded. Collective effervescence involves both will and intention by the collective.

Will and intention are demonstrated in Tahrir Square by the actions and representations indicating Mubarak as the subject of the crowd's fury and by the subsequent celebrations when his resignation is announced. On Wikipedia, the will and intention of the crowd of newcomers descending on the site serve to reinforce this classification. The subsequent title change from "protests" to "revolution" describes a moment of catharsis, of dénouement as the outcome of protests is arrived at and the narrative arc of the event is firmly established and completed. Whereas Wikipedia policy requires an ideal situation in which editors are disconnected and unattached emotionally and physically from the events they are describing, practice indicates that the most important decisions are made by actors who are participants in the same kinds of struggles (and, indeed, may in some cases be protesters themselves).

Crowds come together in both spaces in order to give voice to their collective sentiments and, through the force of their will, to turn events toward the settlement of disruption and the declaration of popular victory. The struggle plays out with historic actors using both words and things[18] to shape the representation of events in both places. Crowds in Tahrir Square and on Wikipedia produce and reproduce symbols that reverberate between one another. This characterizes the realm of discursive action and tactics in both spaces. Important among them is the symbol of Mubarak as the evil son who must be purged from Egypt in order to end the instability and suffering. In Tahrir Square, we see this in the chanting by protesters in response to Mubarak's February 10 speech and the posters that demand his resignation. On Wikipedia, we see it in the discussions that determine Mubarak's resignation as the point at which the article name must change to "revolution."

In Tahrir Square, symbols are generated through the embodied actions and voices of protesters and representations that condense these symbolic actions on the streets. Actions include angrily waving shoes in the air after Mubarak's speech, actively occupying the public square, and declaring victory through celebrations in response to the resignation. Representations include the posters and cartoons, social media reports, and photographs generated and represented in the square.

On Wikipedia, a selection of those actions and symbols are re-presented in the article and in talk page discussions among editors about what is happening. Symbols are also generated through the embodied action using software tactics that aim to alter the core classification of the page and to subvert the actions of those opposing such changes. This is done using coded actions both in the article and on the talk page.

Symbolic action in these places ricochets between one another, across memory and past events, toward the future. Representations in Tahrir Square and on Wikipedia feed off one another. Wikipedia indexes the event by re-presenting particular instances of the narrative: performing as a legitimate copy of events by acting as a summary of "all" representations. Wikipedia's representation of events as a "revolution" is used to signal victory in the authoritative account by protesters and those supporting their actions.

The moment in which the encyclopedic article documenting events in Egypt is changed to "revolution" is the moment when the violence that characterized the previous days, weeks, and years is resolved and made understandable. This historic action signals the moment of triumph for protesters, changing the historical record to reflect their victory and marking an end point to the story of the protests. By naming and serializing, the disruption is settled and a new example is added to the stock of other revolutions throughout history. Similarly, the declaration of victory by protesters enables (relative) calm to return to the square and the country. Such intense emotions cannot be sustained indefinitely, and the celebrations in Tahrir Square signal the end of the disruption.

This moment in the history of the article signals the first end point of a period of great malleability. After this point, the narrative about what happened and why it happened becomes more rigid and inflexible, only able to be shifted after another seismic change. It is at this stage of the event's evolution, in other words, that involvement in the article is most effective. Tariq argues with opposers of the name change that editors can always change the article to another title depending on how events play out in the future. Once a title like revolution stabilizes, though, it takes a significant collective force to rename it.

It is still the case that history is written by the victors. This is a victory of populist politics on Wikipedia, as it is in the streets of Cairo—distinguishing itself from institutional forms of governance on Wikipedia that favor neutrality and a distancing of editors from the subject. It is personal, unmediated by Wikipedia's governing editors and their institutional policies. If Wikipedia is governed by the collective, in this moment it is governed by populist politics rather than the deliberation by all that it aims to achieve. Wikipedia's framing of consensus as achievable via editing enables it to be easily taken over by populist logics, however fleetingly. This is because consensus is determined not by decisions that can be reviewed and accounted for a priori, but by the absence of debate and opposition when there are multiple alternative reasons for the cessation of editing than one's reasoned opposition to the actions of a crowd that forbids control.

Although the classification endures, this victory by the crowd (and by the people in Egypt) is fleeting because it is not connected with the institutional politics that makes change durable. It is fleeting because it is the result of an explosion of intense emotion and attention that cannot be sustained. It is fleeting because, after the fervor that characterizes this moment is over, the collective will necessarily fall back on decision-making according to rules that those governing Wikipedia are able to control.

6

TRANSLATION

EGYPT'S ROCKY ROAD

Celebrations continue in Tahrir Square until the early morning of February 12. Protesters then start to clean up the square. Some pledge to continue protesting until their other demands are met, but the next day, soldiers remove the remaining protesters from Tahrir Square and their tents are dismantled. Regular traffic flows through the square for the first time since the protests began.

Over the next year, Egypt lurches from one crisis to the next. In a failed attempt to quell the protests, Mubarak had named former Egyptian Air Force officer Ahmed Shafiq as prime minister shortly after the unrest began on January 25. But Shafiq is forced to resign the day before mass protests against him are due to take place. Protesters believe that a prime minister sworn in by the ousted leader should not stay in office.

A constitutional referendum proposing a number of reforms, including a limitation on the presidency to no more than two four-year terms, is held in March and passed with a 77 percent majority. Although the reforms are widely recognized as increasing democratic safeguards, opponents like Mohamed ElBaradei and the Coalition of the Youth of the Revolution argue that they don't go far enough. After the Egyptian Cabinet orders a law criminalizing protests and strikes, tens of thousands of protesters return to Tahrir Square to make fresh demands of the military council. Protesters continue to be killed in clashes with security forces.

On June 30, 2012, presidential elections are held, and the Muslim Brotherhood candidate, Mohamed Morsi, is sworn in as Egypt's first democratically elected president. But in November 2012, Morsi issues a declaration immunizing his decrees from challenge. Liberal and secular groups walk out of the constituent assembly, and Morsi's declaration is criticized by Mohamed ElBaradei, who writes on Twitter that the decree effectively places the president above the law, "usurp[ing] all state powers and appoint[ing] himself Egypt's new pharaoh" (@Elbaradei, November 22, 2012).

Protesters again erect tents in Tahrir Square and demand a reversal of the declaration.

DESTINATION: WIKIDATA

After Mubarak's resignation in February 2011, the popularity of the Wikipedia article for readers and editors endures a dramatic decline as attention on events in Egypt dissipates. The hive mind buzzes away to other pages, other events, and other significant occurrences that need to be documented.

The article starts to decay as editors move away en masse. As the websites that editors have linked to restructure their content, the article becomes littered with dead links. Editors may have moved on from the article, but bots continue to do work. In March 2012, DASHbot makes a significant change to the article. For every link to a web page, DASHbot produces a link to that page as it is archived by the Internet Archive, thereby ensuring that there are permanent records for many of the article's hundreds of sources.

The lack of attention by editors results in changes that would have been highly controversial among the cohort editing the article in 2011. In July 2012, the editor SuperHero20111, who did not contribute to the article during events in January and February 2011, proposes on the talk page that the article title be changed. "The revolution began on 25 January 2011, and ended on 30 June 2012," he writes, and suggests the title should be changed from "2011 Egyptian Revolution" to "2011–2012 Egyptian Revolution."[1] The June 30 date refers to Morsi's swearing in as Egypt's first democratically elected president rather than the date when Mubarak resigned. Three editors weigh in to support the move, and SuperHero20111 successfully changes the article title.

It is changed back four months later, when the editor FutureTrillionare suggests that news sources are referring to the "events that led to Mubarak's fall" as the revolution and that events after his fall "are often referred to as 'post-revolution' or 'aftermath' of the revolution." The editor provides five sources as evidence, and eight editors weigh in, mostly to support the move. Lihaas is the only editor who has previously worked on the article offering an opinion. He opposes the move, writing, "A single event does not constitute a revolution" and that Wikipedia "is not a media organization to parrot sensationalism,"[2] but he is in the minority and the change is made despite his opposition.

In November 2012, as Morsi is issuing the decree that immunizes his decisions from challenge, a coup d'état is also achieved on Wikipedia but with little fanfare. On November 12, a bot called MerllwBot creates a record in Wikidata, the newly launched sister site to Wikipedia. This represents one of a series of translations that render Wikipedia's digital information into semantically organized data and package it for distribution through the web. In this way, Wikipedia's classification of events in Egypt is readied for circulation far beyond the Wikipedia domain.

Wikidata is only a few weeks old when this action is taken. Funded in part by Google, Wikidata is the newest project of the Wikimedia Foundation, developed predominantly by Wikimedia Deutschland (Germany). It has two main goals. The first is to help Wikipedia and other Wikimedia projects by ensuring greater consistency across its multiple projects and language versions. The second is to support other (third party) services and applications that want to reuse Wikipedia information. It accomplishes the first goal by acting as a central storage space for the interwiki links that connect different versions of the same article, as well as relevant pages from other Wikimedia projects. It achieves the second goal by collecting data about entities from different Wikimedia projects and placing it in a single authority file.

Wikidata bills itself as a technical project, but it is much more. The creation of items by bots introduces new facts, in addition to reinforcing existing facts. An interwiki link not only plays a functional role for moving users between one language version and another. It is also a statement that two entities (events in this case) are the same.

The Wikidata item for the 2011 Egyptian revolution article links together all its various language versions. Interwiki links assert that the article titled "Egyptian Revolution of 2011" in English Wikipedia, for example, is the same entity as the article titled "Rivoluzione egiziana del 2011" in Italian Wikipedia. They also connect Wikipedia articles about the revolution to data about the revolution in other Wikimedia projects, like Wikinews and Wikiquote.

Wikidata's goal is to develop a semantically organized knowledge base sourced with information from Wikipedia and other Wikimedia Foundation projects, as well as other sources of open data. The knowledge base is unlike traditional databases. Rather than storing data in tables, data is structured—stored as pointers to other objects that, in turn, have additional pointers. On Wikidata, each item (represented by an article on Wikipedia) consists of an identifier, labels, descriptions and aliases in different languages, and a number of statements. The first task for Wikidata when it was launched was to populate its knowledge base with items (for example, people, places, events, and things) and, in turn, to populate those items with objects linking different language versions of the same article.

Wikidata is a source of open data that anyone is free to use under a public domain license. This license enables even more freedoms by downstream users than Wikipedia since, unlike Wikipedia, Wikidata doesn't require its data to be attributed. The licensing of Wikidata under terms that don't require attribution has not been without controversy. Wikipedians like Andreas Kolbe have claimed that this decision was made in order to support Google's wholesale reuse of Wikipedia information without credit.[3] However, others have argued that attribution for facts in databases is both unnecessary and unwieldy; the most important principle is that as many people as possible use Wikidata.

In 2014, I interviewed Max Klein, a longtime Wikipedian and Wikidata editor, about the project. He said that, at first, Wikidata "was basically just an echo chamber of bots talking to each other."[4] When Wikidata first started its work in 2012, some of its editors nicknamed it "Botpedia" because the majority of work was being done by bots designed to import interwiki links and information from infoboxes on Wikipedia.

One of the bots working on Wikidata in its early days was MerllwBot. The English version of the Egyptian revolution article is just one among fifty-seven language versions of the 2011 events when MerllwBot does the work of copying interwiki links from Wikipedia and populating a new item in Wikidata's knowledge base. The trace left by MerllwBot indicates that it has gone to the Lithuanian version of the article, looked for interwiki links, made a copy of those links, and then listed them all under a new item created to house data about the 2011 Egyptian revolution on Wikidata. That item is titled "Q29198," and this serves as its primary identity, connecting multiple sources of data from Wikimedia projects about the revolution, including Wikimedia Commons (where photos of the events are housed).

At this stage, nothing is changed on Wikipedia. The interwiki links in the 2011 Egyptian revolution articles still point to articles within Wikipedia territory. But four months after the Wikidata entity is created for 2011 events in Egypt, the interwiki links on the English version of the article on Wikipedia are removed. Avocato performs the action and summarizes the edit with a comment that the links "already exist in Wikidata."[5]

The interwiki links are thus transcluded. This means that the code that renders the Wikipedia page in your browser makes a call to Wikidata when it wants to display the interwiki links. The data is now housed in Wikidata rather than Wikipedia.

In addition to the primary identity of Q29198 on Wikidata, editors are able to provide secondary descriptors in all the Wikipedia language editions that the article has been created in. This includes a "label" (for example, "2011 Egyptian Revolution"), "description" (at one time, "political upheaval in Egypt, leading to ousting of President Hosni Mubarak"), and "aliases" ("2011–2012 Egyptian revolution," "Revolution of 25 January," "Thawret 25 yanāyir," and "Egyptian revolution of 2011"). These descriptors are curated mostly by human editors who, over the past decade, have added labels, aliases, and descriptions in some of its sixty language versions.

The item also contains what are called "identifiers"—other titles, names, numbers, or combinations of these used for identifying the item in other databases. These include traditional library databases, as well as IDs from

Quora (the US question-and-answer website), IMDb (the Internet Movie Database), and the *Encyclopedia Britannica*. Matching identifiers from other databases is predominantly the work of bots on Wikidata, although human editors, using software tools like Mix'n'Match, help the bot along with items where it doesn't recognize a match.

As statements from Wikipedia are copied across to Wikidata, they are severed from the sources that accompanied them on Wikipedia and attached to new sources. Wikidata has been designed so that each statement can be referenced to a source, thereby upholding Wikipedia's principle of verifiability. But in the decade that I've been studying the article since the item was first created, no human editors have added any references to the properties in the item. The only references that exist are those that have been automatically appended as originating in a particular Wikimedia project or version of Wikipedia (the featured image is one imported from Dutch Wikipedia, for example).

By the beginning of 2020, twenty-four editors and eighteen bots have edited the Wikidata item. Less than a third of the human editors have edited the Wikipedia article before they edit the Wikidata item. Among the editors of both the English Wikipedia and Wikidata items is Aude, the American Wikipedian who was instrumental in negotiating access to Al Jazeera's images for use on Wikipedia in 2011. Aude adds a description in English to the item and an alias. Meno25, who edited the Arabic, Egyptian, and English versions of the article, removes aliases in Arabic and Egyptian Arabic and links the item to its page on Wikiquote in Arabic.

DESTINATION: GOOGLE

Alongside the creation of an Egyptian revolution item on Wikidata in 2012, another significant translation occurs from Wikipedia to Google's newly minted knowledge graph.[6] In a 2012 blog post titled "Things, Not Strings," the senior vice president of engineering for Google, Amit Singhal, writes that Google is using Wikipedia and other "public" data sources to seed a knowledge graph that will provide "smarter search results" for users.[7] Other named sources include the CIA, World Factbook, and Freebase (a now retired online database, formerly owned by Google). In addition to returning a list of possible results—including Wikipedia articles when a user searches for "Marie Curie," for example—Google will present a "knowledge panel" on the right-hand side of the page that "summarize[s] relevant content around that topic, including key facts you're likely to need for that particular thing."[8]

When Google's knowledge graph, using machine learning, brings together billions of entities from around the web that it recognizes as the same person, place, event, or thing, it creates a pool of rich entity data. That data is used to power applications that answer queries by human users speaking to the machine in what linguists and computer scientists call "natural language"—in order to distinguish it from other language types, such as the computing programming languages that provide instructions to machines. In addition to powering knowledge panels on Google's search engine, the knowledge graph is also used to answer spoken voice queries in Google Assistant.

Within seven months of its launch, Google's knowledge graph triples in size to cover 570 entities and 18 billion facts imported from sources like Wikipedia. Results from the graph answer roughly one-third of its 100 billion monthly searches by May 2016. Freebase is shut down in 2016 and its data moved to Wikidata, which then serves as an additional data source for the knowledge graph.

As explained in the first chapter, Wikipedia articles are a prioritized source for Google's featured snippets and knowledge panels, both of which are applications of the knowledge graph. A query for "2011 Egyptian revolution" results in a panel titled "Egyptian revolution of 2011" and provides an opening sentence about the revolution that is cited to Wikipedia, followed by a series of facts summarized into a few words and featured by numbers—the death, injury, and arrest statistics, and the dates of the event—in addition to its location and methods.

Next to the numbers of deaths are the words "See: Deaths section below." But there is no such section below. The phrase is evidence of its extraction from the Wikipedia infobox. On Wikipedia, the phrase is hyperlinked to the section in the article about deaths during the revolution. In Google, there is no hyperlink, and the statement hangs; it is data littering the box.

Although there is a link to Wikipedia after the one-sentence definition drawn from the site, all the other categories imported from Wikipedia now link back to Google's own pages. The location, Cairo, is linked to another Google search for the capital city and an accompanying knowledge panel. So, too, for the "methods" of the revolution, which include "civil disobedience," "demonstration," and "Internet activism." On Wikipedia, these categories are linked to other Wikipedia articles about those subjects, but on Google, clicking the link brings up yet another search result. The foot of Google's knowledge panel contains a list of other entities that "people also search for," including the "Tunisian Revolution," which generates further Google searches.

Soon after Google announces the knowledge graph in May 2012, Dario Taraborelli, former head of research at the Wikimedia Foundation, starts taking notice of how Google represents data from Wikipedia in its knowledge panels. One of the first iterations features a prominent backlink to Wikipedia next to each of the facts under the opening paragraph. There is even reference to the Creative Commons Attribution Share-Alike license that Wikipedia content is licensed under. But, as the panels evolve, blue links to Wikipedia articles start shrinking in size. Over time, the underscore is removed so that the links aren't clickable, and then the links are lightened to a barely visible gray tone. Now, facts under the opening paragraph tend not to be cited at all, and hyperlinked statements refer back to other Google pages.

A PERILOUS JOURNEY

What I've just described is our facts' travel during their most important and perilous journey yet: from the article space of English Wikipedia to a foreign destination, the database. The journey is important because this translation from the article to the database is the way in which classifications in Wikipedia reverberate far beyond their site of production. Wikipedia's authority emerges primarily via the presentation of its facts on third-party sites since most people will encounter Wikipedia's facts about the Egyptian revolution via search engines and digital assistants rather than directly on Wikipedia. The journey is perilous because companions are lost along the way and facts must attract new allies and survive intact after they move to an entirely new environment, subject to new rules and requiring new allies.

Facts' journey from the article to the database is facilitated by algorithms. Algorithms are step-by-step procedures for accomplishing specific tasks or achieving particular goals. The most important algorithms in focus here are those that populate the database and serve results to users' queries. In order to do this work at scale, engineers build ontological models that differentiate between different types of entities, including people, places, events, and things. They might decide, for example, that events in the category "civic disruption" will have start and end dates, or that election events will have a winner and multiple losers. Algorithms govern how data are extracted—and the extent to which their integrity will be retained as they are transported to new environments, since there will always be errors when data doesn't fit the predicted model.

LOST COMPANIONS

Both Wikidata and Google have been accused of discarding sources when extracting facts from Wikipedia articles. Wikidata has been populated by millions of statements that are either uncredited to a reliable source or attributed to the entire Wikipedia language version from where they were extracted. At the end of 2015, about half of Wikidata's statements were unreferenced, and the statements that did have a reference were attributed to a language version of Wikipedia (the English Wikipedia, for example).

Although Wikidata suffers from the loss of source data, it is a public project in which anyone with the means and expertise is able to identify problems and help solve them collectively. Wikimedia volunteers who cared deeply about the importance of verifiability launched the WikiCite project, which uses Wikidata to develop a database of bibliographic data (about published literature, including journal and newspaper articles, books, reports, and patents). But WikiCite focuses primarily on developing source data rather than linking unreferenced statements to sources, and, at the beginning of 2020, about 15 million of the 73 million statements remained unsourced.

Google's knowledge boxes often cite Wikipedia in the opening description of the phenomenon, but the facts following the description remain uncredited. Research conducted by Connor McMahon, Isaac Johnson, and Brent Hecht in 2017 found that facts in the knowledge panels were predominantly sourced from Wikipedia but that these were "almost never cited" and that this was leading to a significant reduction in traffic to Wikipedia.[9] Dario Taraborelli told me that on a few occasions the Wikimedia Foundation and Google have attempted to partner to improve the way in which Wikipedia's brand and attribution are displayed in the knowledge panel. The goal was to remind Google users that these snippets come from a community-run project and that they are the result of the labor of hundreds of thousands of contributors. To his knowledge, though, none of these design proposals or potential partnerships were ever tested or implemented in production.[10] In 2021, the Wikimedia Foundation launched a new commercial product, Wikimedia Enterprise, for large-scale reusers and distributors of Wikimedia content. Designed for companies and organizations who want to reuse content more easily from Wikipedia and Wikimedia projects at a high volume, it is hoped that Wikimedia Enterprise will enable Wikimedia to claw back some of the resources they have lost in the widescale commercial extraction of knowledge that volunteers have produced.

NEW ALLIES

Another feature of the translation from the article to the database is that facts become governed by a new set of allies. Until now, facts' allies have been dominated by human editors, but their transfer to Wikidata and Google is achieved predominantly by automated agents and the engineers who create them.

Google's knowledge graph is populated by facts that are extracted, prioritized, and presented by algorithmic systems developed by engineers across multiple teams at Google. After being trained on a data set that is structured by human oversight, those systems start to learn independently how to recognize that a piece of data from one location is the same entity as one from another location, and they automatically mash up data from multiple sources. Given that the systems start to operate independently, human users (even those who created those systems) lose agency in controlling the representation of the data.

For example, in late 2017, Rachel Abrams's father googled his daughter and found that she was dead.[11] Abrams is a *New York Times* columnist, and a Google search had an image of her next to the details of another writer with the same name who died in 2013. Abrams tried submitting feedback through Google's automated system. She then emailed Google's corporate communications team regarding her problem, saying that she was from the media. The spokesperson wrote back with a link to a help page, but none of the options provided were applicable to her as "the authority on her self."

After eventually reaching someone at the Googleplex in Mountain View, California, she was advised to "keep submitting feedback, over and over again from different IP addresses." Doing so would teach the algorithm automating the results that her content was more accurate, and it would rise to the top of Google's search rankings.

Even though Wikidata's entities are open for public scrutiny and editing, many Wikipedia editors lose their ability to make meaningful changes to the facts that they constructed once they move to Wikidata. As it turns out, editing a semantic database requires very different expertise, and the ways in which editors think about the topics that they edit are different still. Some Wikipedia editors complain that articles are being edited remotely, that the edits are being made without reliable sources because the algorithm can't evaluate the reliability of sources (and doesn't consider whether a statement has a source attached to it as grounds for its quality) before extracting them. The edits don't show up on editors' watch lists automatically, and sometimes incorrect information is on display for months before anyone notices.

In one example, the Wikipedian SarahSV gave grounds for opposing a Wikipedia RFC (request for comment) about the extent to which Wikidata should control English Wikipedia infoboxes.[12] SarahSV wrote about her misgivings using the example of an article about the book *Night,* which she had been editing. *Night* is about Elie Wiesel's time in concentration camps with his father during the Holocaust. SarahSV noticed that the infobox was suddenly listing the genre as "autobiographical novel" when she had previously left the field empty. She had done so because scholars couldn't agree on the genre, and Holocaust deniers call it a novel in their efforts to fictionalize it.

SarahSV investigated and realized that a Wikidata bot had copied the genre data (that it was an "autobiographical novel") from Italian Wikipedia, where it was classified as a novel. Because the English Wikipedia infobox had no field for genre, the Wikidata algorithm, seeing this as missing information that needed to be filled in, unhelpfully added the translated field to it, thereby undoing SarahSV's careful efforts.

The problem, wrote SarahSV, was that she couldn't work out how to remove it, and it "wasn't easy to see when the change had been made; when I looked through the article history, the Wikidata addition was showing up in old versions of the article."[13]

NEW LAWS

The third feature of the journey from Wikipedia to the new territory of the semantic database is that facts are subject to new rules and laws. The issue here is that the laws of these new lands are constituted by voids and obscurity, and this is especially the case when they are first launched. Both Wikidata and Google began their work building their algorithmic systems with a focus on computational rules for deciding when two entities are alike, but not on rules for deciding among competing factual claims or for thinking about quality of sources or their verifiability.

Wikidata's policies on notability and verifiability lay untouched for years before they were developed. Whereas Wikipedia highlights its rules and policies about content creation as critical to learn before one starts editing, Wikidata's entry points to editing begin with editors immediately tasked with adding missing labels and descriptions.

Unlike Wikipedia, which is developed and discussed by editors in almost three hundred languages, Wikidata discussions happen in English. As a result, Wikidata suffers from diminished opportunities for debate and contestation at a local or regional level. Shortly after Wikidata was founded, my supervisor at Oxford, Mark Graham, wrote in the *Atlantic* that it was a problem that "a disagreement over facts or data would no longer be confined to a specific article and language, but would most likely have to be conducted in English to an unfamiliar community of editors."[14] He wrote that Wikidata was significant because, until the project was launched, Wikipedia had never attempted to develop consistency across all languages.

Look, for instance, at the Wikipedia pages about the Bronze Statue of Tallinn (a highly controversial moment in Estonia's history that sparked one of the world's first "cyberwars" between Russia and Estonia). The Estonian and Russian versions of that article present interestingly different versions of the very same place and events. The Arabic and Hebrew articles about Hezbollah offer perhaps an even starker contrast of the ways in which different communities of editors agree on different types of representation and truths.

For those who are literate in the workings of Wikidata and who have some command of English, there are opportunities to improve the rules by which data is represented. For example, Max Klein, the Wikidata editor I spoke to in 2014, talked about how he had contributed to rules about how the "sex or gender" property worked on Wikidata.

When I came across it, the "sex or gender" property said "only one of 'male, female, or intersex'." I was opposed to this because I believe that any way the Wikidata community structure the gender options, we are going to imbue it with our own bias. For instance, already the property is called "sex or gender," which shows a lack of distinction between the two, which some people would consider important. So I spent some time arguing that at least we should allow any value. So if you want to say that someone is "third gender" or even that their gender is "Sodium" that's now possible. It was just an early case of heteronormativity sneaking into the ontology.[15]

In contrast, the opportunities for debating mistakes on Google's platform are nonexistent. Over the past eight years, the process by which users can suggest fixes to knowledge panels has hardly changed, even while Google's representation of facts has grown exponentially. In 2012, users were able to provide "feedback" by clicking a button labeled "wrong?" on each of the fields of the panel. Eight years later, the only difference is that users must provide information about "what is wrong with this" (this was optional before).

No information is available about what happens to a user's feedback once they've provided it, and there is no response to that feedback beyond Google stating that it will not change the results. After the user submits feedback, Google makes clear that "your feedback will help improve Google search results" but that "the feedback you give won't influence a page's ranking in results." It is difficult to understand the logic of improving results without influencing them. Google seems to be saying that users can provide the kind of feedback that will help the company provide a better service (as they define it), while reminding individuals that they don't really have much agency in actually changing the results if they are false.

We are free labor for Google's algorithms rather than subjects of facts represented there.

Google now provides the opportunity for making a "legal removal request," which could be useful when laws exist to protect individuals and groups from harm. It also provides the opportunity for claiming panels by those who "are the subject or official representative of an entity depicted." This may be useful to corporations that are able to fulfill Google's requirements for identity verification. But for ordinary users or communities of users without official identity markers, attempting to provide meaningful feedback about incorrect representations in the knowledge panel is a meaningless gesture.

Both Google's and Wikidata's coups over facts from Wikipedia represent a change in governance that is characterized by voids and obscurity, but there are significant differences between the two. Whereas the algorithmic systems that translate Wikipedia facts to the Google knowledge graph are hidden, the rules by which facts are translated from Wikipedia and other Wikimedia sites to Wikidata are visible to any user by visiting MerllwBot's user page and looking at its source code. Claims made in both Wikidata and Wikipedia can be questioned and debated, whereas on Google, responses by users are limited essentially to voting—but where the rules by which votes are calculated are obscured, and users are told that their actions won't result in change in any case.

THE PROBLEM OF PROVENANCE

The translation from digital to semantic data—from the article to the database—is an enormous achievement. It enables datafied facts and the classifications that they represent to travel much farther from their origins and to influence what becomes recognized as common knowledge. But there are risks to translation by automation. Information loss can cause the integrity of facts to degrade, meaning is lost or altered, and opportunities for debate and consensus building, however thin, are significantly reduced.

I have argued in other forums that the loss of source data, in particular, introduces Wikipedia's greatest existential threat to date.[16] This is not just because of the ways in which third-party actors appropriate Wikipedia content and remove the links that might sustain the community in terms of contributions of donations and volunteer time. More important is that unsourced Wikipedia content threatens the principle of verifiability, one of the fundamental principles on which Wikipedia was built.

After he noticed that the Google knowledge panels were removing citations to Wikipedia, Dario Taraborelli became concerned at how dependent Wikipedia was on Google, and at how changes being made to the way that Google presented Wikipedia content could have a significant impact on the sustainability of Wikipedia.[17] If users were being presented with information from Wikipedia without having to visit the site or without even knowing that Wikipedia was the true source, that would surely affect the numbers of users visiting Wikipedia—as readers, editors, or contributors to the annual fund-raising campaign.

Taraborelli was also concerned with a more fundamental principle—that Google's use of Wikipedia information without credit "undermines people's ability to verify information and, ultimately, to develop well-informed opinions."[18] And, as we have seen, verifiability is one of Wikipedia's core content policies.

Verifiability sets up a series of rights and obligations by readers and editors of Wikipedia. Readers have a right to information on Wikipedia that they can check via the original source; editors have an obligation to provide citations for statements to enable these rights. By removing direct links to the Wikipedia article where statements originate from, search engines and digital assistants are removing the clues that allow readers to evaluate the veracity of claims and take active steps to change that information through consensus if they feel that it is false.

What is interesting is that provenance was actually a key feature of earlier visions of the semantic web that served as antecedents for current projects like Wikidata and Google's knowledge graph. According to the World Wide Web Consortium, provenance is "a record that describes the people, institutions, entities, and activities involved in producing, influencing, or delivering a piece of data or a thing in the world."[19] The W3C, as it is known, is the primary international standards organization for the World Wide Web. Founded in 1994 and led by the inventor of the web, Tim Berners-Lee, the consortium works to develop standards for the web.

In 1997, Berners-Lee gave a talk in London at the W3C, where he shared his vision for moving from a web of information produced for and by humans to a web of machine-understandable information where the "trade and bureaucracy" would be handled by automated agents, leaving humans to provide the "inspiration and the intuition."

Fundamental to this transfer of authority to agents was an ability to question that authority. Berners-Lee imagined this questioning in terms of an "Oh yeah?" button on one's browser. Pressing the button meant that "you are asking your browser why you should believe it." This would constitute a "challenge" to the server to provide some credentials that might help you trust the information you're reading.

Four years later, Berners-Lee and coauthors wrote an article for the *Scientific American* titled "The Semantic Web."[20] Instead of information being developed for human consumption, the authors argued that it needed to be restructured so that machines could more efficiently deliver personalized results and services. Optimistically, they wrote that the web was moving away from the "web of documents" and the storing of data in flat, static formats and moving toward the abstraction of information into short, modular statements that could be linked together and mined by algorithmic processes that would better enable "computers and people to work in cooperation." They elaborated on the issue of data provenance as a key feature of the vision:

> An important facet of agents' functioning will be the exchange of "proofs" written in the Semantic Web's unifying language (the language that expresses logical inferences made using rules and information such as those specified by ontologies). For example, suppose [someone's] contact information has been located by an online service, and to your great surprise it places [them] in Johannesburg. Naturally, you want to check this, so your computer asks the service for a proof of its answer, which it promptly provides by translating its internal reasoning into the Semantic Web's unifying language.

Another important feature would be digital signatures to verify that attached information was being provided by a trusted source: "Agents should be skeptical of assertions that they read on the Semantic Web until they have checked the sources of information."

Since then, the technical community has shown great enthusiasm for provenance. A W3C working group on provenance has developed PROV, a specification that provides a technical vocabulary to exchange provenance information. They argue that provenance is important because it has always been a fundamental tenet of the scientific method, capturing all the steps involved in deriving a particular result, enabling others to follow the steps in order to test or validate those results.

The journalistic community, too, continually calls for greater provenance. Journalism professor and writer Jeff Jarvis writes about the importance of provenance for news in order to accord credit (and sometimes financial value) to the source. It enables readers to develop trust and to evaluate and dig deeper into sources, and it allows journalists to take responsibility.

It appears that provenance is crucial to individuals when deciding whether information is to be trusted and for giving credit to its originators when reusing data. Despite this, computer scientists like Mike Bergman, when defining knowledge graphs, note that they do not strictly require provenance and context, although both are useful.[21] As a result, contrary to Tim Berners-Lee's original hopes, provenance has not been baked into current systems.

FROM TRANSPARENCY TO ACCOUNTABILITY

I've joined others in arguing that surfacing source information for facts in algorithmic systems like Google's knowledge graph is important. But how *should* sources be referred to? Those who have opposed Google's actions in the past (me included) have stressed the importance of linking back to Wikipedia generally. There are two problems with a simple link back to Wikipedia as a solution to the problem if increased verifiability is the goal.

First, surfacing information about which Wikipedia article facts are extracted from, in order to furnish Google's knowledge panels, is meaningless unless there is information about when and how it was extracted. Wikipedia articles are subject to vandalism, and although this act is often fixed in minutes, if the information was extracted after the article was altered, then going to the Wikipedia article to make the change will not help fix the mistake until facts are updated.

Facts on Wikipedia also contain contextual information that adds significantly to their meaning. When an editor adds a "citation needed" template to a statement, readers know that they cannot fully trust the accuracy of the statement. The breaking news template warns readers that information in an article is rapidly changing in the context of a breaking news event.

Information about how data is extracted is similarly important. There are already differences between Wikipedia and Wikidata in their representation of entities, and we don't know how Google reconciles those differences, as it identifies both Wikipedia and Wikidata as prioritized sources. Without this information, those who bring problems to light in the media (since they have no relief with Google) can only guess.

A second problem with linking back to Wikipedia is that even if people follow that link, it isn't guaranteed that they will discover the original source of a fact or learn how the decision to display this information (rather than its alternatives) was made. As discussed in previous chapters, the source supplied on Wikipedia isn't always the original source, and not all statements on Wikipedia have sources appended to them.

As I showed in the discussion of the classification of the *Night* book, high levels of subject matter expertise are required to uncover why some infobox entries appear as they do when they are generated from within the Wikidata domain. And the decision-making processes are not always available either. Also, editors sometimes remove citations when they believe that statements have become common knowledge, commonly accepted as the "truth," even though other editors (or others outside Wikipedia) may reject that assumption. Making visible the path back from Google to Wikipedia, in other words, does not necessarily result in the ability of users to check where information comes from.

Mike Ananny and Kate Crawford write about the limitations of viewing the transparency solution as a type of accountability in algorithmic systems, or that seeing inside an algorithmic system will instantly lead to it being called to account: "The assumption behind calls for transparency is that seeing a phenomenon creates opportunities and obligations to make it accountable and thus to change it."[22]

Actually, there are significant limitations to transparency as a mechanism for holding powers to account. Despite researchers uncovering evidence that facts in knowledge panels are, indeed, from Wikipedia, Google has not made any moves to alter its practices. Calls for transparency often don't account for the massive power differentials between actors. They ignore the fact that Google will not instantly become more accountable to those whose information it consumes and presents as its own, or to those it ultimately represents as subjects of that information. Google is not accountable because it doesn't have to be.

All knowledge work involves an interplay between tacit and explicit knowledge, formal and informal knowledge. Ananny and Crawford write that sometimes there are interests in making systems appear to be transparent, when actually they obscure how much editing work is not about the formal application of a consistent, reliable sources policy but is the result of an interplay between a number of factors that results in a great deal of informal knowledge being applied. Similarly, listing Wikipedia as the source of statements adds to the illusion that having a cited source produces instant transparency about the practices of editing, when actually those practices are still obscure.

Even if users are able to see source information next to each fact in the knowledge panel, this will not instantly increase their ability or motivation to go to Wikipedia and change it. The focus on transparency as a type of accountability has led to systems that reveal important information about a product, service, or system as a way for individuals to change their behavior in relation to it. Seeing inside a can of Coke by listing its sugar content was assumed to lead to the knowledge and awareness necessary for individuals to drink less of it or to stop drinking it altogether.

Ananny and Crawford warn against this approach, arguing that a focus on transparency as the primary vehicle for accountability assumes the active participation of individuals interested in and able to provide oversight. In many cases, though, individuals do not have the motivations, skills, or associations to achieve this oversight. There is also the problem that placing the burden on individuals to solve the problem belies the systematic nature of the problem and the need for collective forms of oversight in order to achieve true accountability.

Similarly, revealing source information in knowledge panels does not necessarily mean that users will be motivated to check whether that information is accurate. Researchers observing the behavior of users on automated systems indicate that they don't question information that is algorithmically derived.[23] Wikipedia users generally don't look at or follow up on the validity of sources. Even if people were motivated to visit Wikipedia to debate a statement presented as fact, there is a high barrier to entry for Wikipedia editing, especially in controversial subjects. Successful Wikipedia editing is available only to the few willing to undertake the time and emotional labor necessary for the task.

Despite all the limitations of the transparency ideal, there is still significant value in appending source information to statements in the knowledge graph. Wikipedia depends on links back to the site for its future sustainability, and Wikimedia sites including Wikipedia and Wikidata provide much thicker mechanisms for accountability and greater opportunities to debate and discuss contentious issues than Google allows or can be trusted with facilitating. But if source information is to be surfaced, then we need to think carefully about surfacing the contexts of its extraction as well. Critical among this contextual information is temporality (when information was extracted) and the stability or instability of information if it is subject to current events and controversies.

This effort needs to be undertaken with the knowledge that verifiability won't necessarily lead to the immediate accountability of Google, Wikipedia, or Wikidata. Improving evidence of the trail that facts follow when they are ingested and then regurgitated by automated systems may actually strengthen the public's unfounded trust in automated systems. Constantly improving mechanisms for people to speak back to the data that affects their well-being, their identity, and their sense of political agency should be the ultimate goal, rather than the transparency of the system itself.

7

TOWARD PEOPLE'S HISTORIES

I last talked to The Egyptian Liberal in February 2017.[1] We talk on Skype. The disappointment is thick in his voice—so different from the youthful, insistent voice I had spoken to immediately after the revolution.

"The stupidity that the human race is exhibiting blows my mind," he says sadly. "The backlash by the new government was unbelievable. It happened during eighteen days . . . against anyone who was young, who was participating. The older generation did a number on the younger generation in Egypt."

The Egyptian Liberal tells other activists in Egypt to read the Wikipedia article to get the full story of what happened. "The articles created out of the events in Egypt on English Wikipedia were once considered an excellent source of information about what was happening in Egypt. Some of the articles are still good," muses Liberal.

> But the revolution article became more opinionated. People thought differently. There was a lot of propaganda . . . people being paid by the government to edit. People can't agree on anything. Having one goal is easier than having different goals. Despite the fact that not a lot of people in Egypt can read English and the Arabic version of the article is weak, there is the problem that people all have their own experience of the revolution and no amount of facts will help them to change their minds about it. They don't read it because they experienced it. They lived it.

For those who experienced the revolution in the streets of Egypt, the facts created about it are secondary to the knowledge that comes from their witnessing of history. That knowledge is still most powerful. Before and after facts there are stories—stories that are deeply embedded in the psyches of those who experienced events, who were inside the event, close to its nucleus.

For those who documented the event as it happened on Wikipedia, the experience of working together as witnesses to history is also distinct from the facts that endure on the page. A few months later, Ocaasi and I are sitting in the lounge of a budget hotel in the outskirts of Vienna. We've been participating in a WikiCite conference.

I ask him how he now thinks about the Wikipedia article in which he played such an important role.

> It changed my life. It's the most I've ever been engaged intellectually, the most connected I've ever been to world politics; the most hopeful I've ever been about the possibility for people to determine their own fate and governance . . . before that on Wikipedia was just playing around and this was not. It was also when my innocence about Wikipedia ended. . . . I thought the world mattered so much those days and I thought I could play a part—not in an activist sense but by documenting what was happening.
>
> It was very personal for me. . . . It wasn't about geopolitics or civic engagement. It was about these figures—Bouazizi who had lost his dignity and set himself on fire; Kahled Saeed who was battered by the police. Those incidents and the response that people had to those incidents made me feel like good could conquer evil. And that faith that if you fight against evil, you will prevail did happen in the Egyptian Revolution. But that the opposite of war isn't peace it's creation. Throwing out the bad guy isn't even half the battle.[2]

For Ocaasi, there is still hope. "There's nothing more powerful than being part of a dedicated group of people trying to change the world," he told me. "And I got a glimpse of that from Wikipedia. I don't have a global faith. I have a local faith in my community and the work that we do."

The Egyptian Liberal and Ocaasi were two people bearing witness to history: both inside the event, despite the thousands of miles that separated them. Close in age, they established a firm connection during the revolution as they experienced an event that shook the world for ten days in early 2011. The 2011 Egyptian revolution had enormous effects that we are still grappling with today—not only the political and social consequences but also the personal effects for those documenting the event in a small but significant corner of the internet.

Ocaasi went on to a successful career working for the Wikimedia Foundation after he founded the Wikipedia Library project. I don't know where The Egyptian Liberal is or what he is doing now. He no longer responds to my emails. For him, the failure of the revolution means so much more. When I spoke to him last, he had no hope left, although he obviously recognized the important role that he played in documenting events for the world from inside Egypt.

EVENTS AS DATA

History is written by the victors. But who are the victors in the face of wide-scale datafication of knowledge and the representation of events in the minutes, hours, and days after they unfold? Does Wikipedia enable us to write "the people's history," collaboratively, by consensus and driven by human knowledge? Or is the result a "certain people's history," driven by machines and unaccountable to the people who create it? If there are weaknesses in our internet infrastructure that prevent consensus building, what are they and what can we do to strengthen them?

Questions about who gets to write the first draft of history and the role of the media are enduring ones. In 1992, Daniel Dayan and Elihu Katz explored the role of television in the live broadcasting of historic events like the Olympic Games, the wedding of Prince Charles and Lady Diana, and the funeral of John F. Kennedy. Their book, *Media Events*,[3] was pathbreaking because it demonstrated the transforming power of the live television broadcast.

Media technology, argued Dayan and Katz, had the potential to transform "not only a 'message,' not only the nature of response, but an entire structure of social relations."[4] Historic events, broadcast on television to transfixed viewers around the world, served as unifying rituals. Everyone gathered around their television screens to engage in the collective viewing of a single event, coproduced by broadcasters and their state partners.

In 1992, it seemed impossible for historic events to have any public meaning without their transmission by television broadcasting. Today, it is impossible for historic events to have any public meaning without their transmission as *data*. In contrast to news reports, books, documentaries, and other fact-based media, event data is a powerful representative force because it can travel most fruitfully to reach massive audiences and because of its prize location as the single answer to user queries on the web.

Today, terrorist attacks, natural disasters, protests, and pandemics—incidents and accidents—have added to the weddings, funerals, and sporting events that Dayan and Katz wrote about in 1992. The events that seem to arise daily and upend our societies are unexpected rather than expected. Rather than unifying societies through their single narrative arc, media events today are characterized by a fracturing of voices that compete to determine the meaning of what happened. In addition to television broadcasters, a myriad of actors across digital platforms are documenting historic events as they happen. The authority to determine the significance and meaning of the event, as well as its geographical scope, has been fundamentally altered.[5]

The dominant conception of Wikipedia is that the knowledge it produces is the end result of negotiation, guided by the principle of consensus on which the site was founded. As a result, Wikipedia reflects "common knowledge"[6] and "collective memory."[7] When we hear about history making on Wikipedia, authors often rely on Wikipedia's own explanations of how articles are constructed: according to a neutral point of view and the result of consensus.

Investigating the life of a single Wikipedia article and its data puts these accounts in doubt. Rather than negotiation and consensus, Wikipedia articles about historic events like the Egyptian revolution are characterized by agonistic encounters. There are many different ways of seeing the world. Knowledge is always multiple. There will always be an inevitable conflict between those tasked with its representation, especially when the risks and rewards are so great.

Event stakeholders struggle to shape the meaning of critical events using the tools (weapons) at their disposal. Their goal is to influence event data, the most powerful representations. The resultant struggles reflect new tactics of power and knowledge.

Today, the multiple meanings of events are visible in discussions and debates about their representation across platforms of knowledge, including on Wikipedia, where many of these struggles are permanently archived. Skirmishes over the meaning of events are ramped up by the forces that would have them represented as simplified (and often singular) data about events. The web has catalyzed a host of representations by journalists, citizens, civil society, and state actors via social media and digital platforms. The battle over event data has intensified.

To many, the brute force of the algorithm in translating the meaning of events means that human history making has been ceded to automated technologies. "Where history was once written by its victors, and later by its nerds, it's now being shaped by its algorithms," wrote *Washington Post* journalist Caitlyn Dewey in an article about Google's knowledge panels and their rapidly disappearing Wikipedia data sources.[8]

But as described in the previous pages, forces both internal and external to Wikipedia help shape data representations of the event that later inhabit the knowledge graph. Internal forces include Wikipedians and Wikipedia's classification technologies. External forces include sources, crowds, and algorithms. Importantly, they also include the event itself. The defining characteristic of unplanned historic events is that there is an information vacuum and a corresponding need for publics to obtain information in order to ease the sense of dis-ease. Events in Egypt in January 2011 drove crowds to the Wikipedia article on waves of media attention. They influenced the market of sources available to Wikipedia editors.

The resulting representations are not an indication of *everyone's* memory or meaning of what happened. Particular types of actors are more suited to the rapid retelling of events in real time and according to the logics of data. The form and temporality of the representations that dominate our knowledge of what happened have implications for who has the power to influence them.

Data about events as they happen, created by a distributed group of individuals and technologies, may appear to be a supremely efficient way of producing knowledge. But there are dangers when facts are accorded this much power, largely driven by the framings of their American hosts and weaknesses in the infrastructure that could leave them vulnerable to manipulation.

CROWDS, INVISIBLE RULES, AND UNFETTERED POWER: WEAKNESSES OF INTERNET INFRASTRUCTURE

The first weakness of our knowledge infrastructures is their vulnerability to crowds driven by collective emotion in the moments and days after historic events. Wikipedia is the first encyclopedia to narrate historic events as they happen and is vulnerable to decisions driven by the emotion (whether it is euphoria or vengeance) and violence of the crowd. As a result, the actions of crowds can result in a loss of accountability on Wikipedia because they cannot be traced back to a particular discussion or consensus-building exercise. Decisions at the crucial moment in which performative utterances are made (for example, "I resign") result in a crowd moving into the article, compelled by their desire to make history, rather than to deliberate with others.

The second weakness is the vulnerability of facts to the obscure actions of algorithms that results in a loss of transparency in facts' origins. When facts are translated into semantic data and moved from their source, they shed the traces of their origins—including their companions (sources) as well as traces of the decision-making processes by which they were made. Wikipedia does a good job of citing statements, especially contentious ones. Wikidata, on the other hand, suffers from a significant lack of source information. Many factual statements are cited to the Wikipedia language edition from where they were automatically extracted, rather than to the reliable source that informed them.

Although Wikipedia's talk pages and edit histories make a noteworthy proportion of the decision-making processes technically available, transparency is hampered by two factors. First is the trace literacy needed in order to decipher complex decisions that take place across the talk pages and edit histories of articles. Second is the fact that some decisions are made outside of deliberative processes (such as the article's name change from "protests" to "revolution").

On Google, the lack of transparency is significantly more dire. Facts in the knowledge graph often lack source information, which makes it impossible for users to know the origin of those facts. There is also a lack of transparency in how one factual statement is selected over others or how statements can be changed if they are incorrect or misleading. Knowledge graphs were developed with a focus on computational rules rather than rules that deal with the inevitable ambiguity of knowledges, especially unstable ones, developed in the context of rapidly evolving political events.

The automation of facts from Wikipedia to the knowledge graphs in both Wikidata and Google can result in information loss that substantially changes the meaning of events and creates a situation where false or misleading information is difficult (sometimes impossible) for users to fix. Difficult in the case of Wikidata, because facts are now housed within a completely new environment of the database that is unknown to or not understood by Wikipedians and that is dominated by new rules and logics. Impossible in the case of Google, because there is no way for users to make changes, apart from making suggestions according to invisible rules and processes.

Every translation of datafied facts from Wikipedia to the knowledge graph results in a coup d'état by engineers and their attendant algorithms, where the governance of facts is imposed by technical rules rather than deliberative principles and where the importance of facts for deciding the distribution of power and resources is ignored.

Despite their weaknesses, platforms like Wikipedia and Google enjoy significant authority and obedience. Wikipedia's authority emerges, in part, because it seems to represent global consensus. If Wikipedia enables multiple voices to gather together to settle their differences, then the result will be an eradication of bias, a settling into the so-called wisdom of crowds. Facts in Google's knowledge graph, for example, appear to be accurate because they come from Wikipedia (where the logic of the crowd dominates) and are subject to automated mechanisms when they are provided as answers to questions on search engines, digital assistants, or smart speakers.

The lack of source information reinforces their authority still further. Facts presented this way use the same "god trick" as the scientific objectivity that Donna Haraway wrote about in the late 1980s United States because they distance the source of knowledge "from everybody and everything in the interests of unfettered power."[9] It is this unquestioned authority in only a very few platforms, all hosted in the United States, that constitutes the third weakness in our knowledge infrastructure.

A RENEWED FOCUS ON SITUATING DATA

The loss of information about where facts come from and how decisions about them were made leaves Wikipedia, Wikidata, and Google vulnerable to both unintentional inaccuracies (misinformation) and intentional activities aimed at deception (disinformation). Even more important, it leaves these platforms apparently omniscient.

These problems won't be solved by any single company or any single state. One thing is certain, though: we can no longer invest all our resources in solving these problems through debiasing initiatives, usually conducted by platforms independently and privately, outside of the purview of the communities whom they ultimately represent.

Instead, knowledge platforms need to provide contextual clues to the knowledge that they currently present as the single, objective truth about what happened. And they need to improve their governance procedures so that they are more inclusive of those who are most affected by those representations.

Situating data requires embracing design principles that foreground the ways in which facts were produced and by whom they were produced and highlighting the volatility of information affected by historic events. Knowledge graphs that display a single answer to users' queries, often without the source being visible, can highlight the origin of facts and their paths to the knowledge graph in ways that surface the knowing subject. This includes finding ways of attributing both the source and the rules or assumptions that are made in determining the prioritized, single answer to users' queries. This may seem unwieldy for a form that aspires to simplicity, but there will certainly be creative ways to design such reflexivity into automated systems.

Perhaps this is simply about being able to question the knowledge graph about the origins of the facts displayed—an option that would work for both search engines and digital assistants. Instead of only being able to ask "What happened on January 6, 2021, in Washington, DC?" we also need to be able to ask search engines and digital assistants "How can you be certain?"

Reflexive systems should also be able to flag the instability of facts in the early days of an unexpected, historic event. We need new ways of sensing instability (according to the behavior of crowds on platforms and waves of media attention) and new grammars to draw attention to facts' volatility. Wikipedians flag articles to warn users that the article is the subject of a breaking news event. But there is currently no equivalent when facts are rendered in Google's knowledge graph or on Wikidata.

Instead of engineering systems to automatically label facts as either true or false, platform infrastructures could invest in flagging facts as stable or unstable. Such representations would situate knowledges in ways that enable greater user agency than an automated platform deciding for those users what is true or false.

Although some of these principles can be achieved by design, much more needs to be done to improve the accountable governance of platforms that house and curate our knowledge about the world. Wikipedia, Wikidata, and Google all need to improve the ways in which they are governed in order to support that accountability. For articles affected by historic events, Wikipedia and Wikidata need to develop policies that support slower deliberation in the face of crowds that would rather make decisions impulsively. Although Wikipedia has significant defenses against vandals acting as individuals or even small groups, it cannot defend itself against the actions of large crowds. Two things remain to be seen: whether Wikipedians can sanction the crowds that they are also ultimately still so dependent on, and whether they can translate the importance of verifiability in the age of the knowledge graph as their labor is increasingly extracted by automated platforms without credit.

Companies that operate knowledge graphs (including those operated by Google but also Apple, Amazon, Facebook, and LinkedIn) need to make the rules by which they select and alter facts in the knowledge graph publicly available. They need to commit to (and be audited on) principles of attribution and algorithmic transparency that leave the attribution to Wikipedia (and other sources) intact.

These actions will not take place without significant public pressure. Public data literacy, then, is a crucial component of any solution to keep platforms accountable. People around the world rely on knowledge platforms to make decisions not only as consumers but also as citizens. Data literacy is core to the concept of digital citizenship. It involves the knowledge of how factual data are constructed and how to write them into being on particular platforms. Crucially, though, data literacy also requires an understanding of how a single platform feeds into a much larger system in which datafied facts travel. This is about understanding what the points of weakness are, who is actually in charge (even when it appears no one is), at which points in time is knowledge most vulnerable, and how algorithms work to simplify information that comes at the cost of a change in their meaning.

* * *

I began the story of events in Egypt in 2011 with the actions of a single Wikipedia editor, born in Egypt and driven by a hope that he could change the world. The story started off as malleable, peopled, available for transformation. But it ended up very rapidly closed off to debate and politics.

What is required now is a reopening of spaces for debate and politics but within the bounds of new territories in which algorithms and crowd logics currently reign supreme. As computers gain new abilities to talk to each other through the translation of knowledge into data, we need new, human grammars for attending to the politics of facts in a world that is being constantly shaken by the force of critical events.

A focus of these grammars should be on the ability of automated systems to "situate knowledges," in Donna Haraway's terms: to give context to facts by surfacing the details of their social and technical production. Facts, as we must continually remind ourselves, are human made. Despite our enhanced abilities to construct them using new tools, we have the ability to remake those tools to serve the publics they ultimately work for.

If we do not, we will continue to trick ourselves into believing that, if we try just a little harder and obtain just a little more information, we can reflect all human knowledge in a single frame. There can be no representation outside a frame. The best we can hope for is to at least make the frames visible.

ACKNOWLEDGMENTS

Research for this book took me almost a decade. During that time, I lived in the United States and the United Kingdom, and now I live in Australia. I have been lifted on the shoulders of so many people during my own tumultuous times.

I first became interested in Wikipedia as a research site while completing my master's degree at the School of Information at the University of California, Berkeley. Jenna Burrell was instrumental in my decision to become an ethnographer, and Deidre Mulligan gave me vital research experience while I was a student there. Toward the end of my master's degree, I read a blog post by Ethan Zuckerman about the Kenyan superhero character Makmende and attempts by Kenyan Wikipedians to include an article about the character and its attendant meme that was becoming recognized as Kenya's first internet meme. This inspired me to write my very first article about Wikipedia, which I presented at a small conference in Bangalore called Critical Point of View. CPOV brought together researchers in a critical reflection on the emergence of Wikipedia in the contexts of education, politics, resistance, and knowledge production. Led by Geert Lovinck and Nathaniel Tkacz, the network laid the foundation for my future critical research on Wikipedia. I am eternally grateful to Ethan, Geert, and Nate for inspiring me on this decade-long trajectory to understand Wikipedia from a very different POV.

I'm grateful, too, to Ushahidi for giving me my first break as an ethnographer in 2012 and for allowing me the opportunity to study the Egyptian revolution article on Wikipedia as an example of how accounts of political events can be verified on social media in real time. Mark Graham and Eric Meyer at the Oxford Internet Institute were indispensable in their support of my early research on Wikipedia, as the first pages of the book indicate. Mark invited me to be a part of his study of Wikipedia in the Middle East and coauthored several papers with me before I graduated. Eric pointed me to the literature on the travel of facts and helped me found a new ethnography group, the Oxford Digital Ethnography Group, where I honed my ethnographic practice while at Oxford.

I am grateful to the collaborators with whom I have worked on related Wikipedia research projects, including Stuart Geiger, Shilad Sen, David Musicant, Brent Hecht, Oliver Keyes, and the inimitable Judy Wajcman. Thanks also to those who I haven't necessarily shared a byline with (yet) but who have been a font of support, including Jodi Schneider, who never stopped sending relevant articles and useful information to me throughout this period.

At Leeds University I was lucky to find kindred spirits in Stephen Coleman and Lone Sorensen, who helped me think about the mediation of historic events in new ways. Bethany Klein read early and late drafts of my work and offered encouragement and support when I most needed it.

At the end of 2018, I left Leeds to join my partner in Australia. In the final years of writing this book, I was offered space by numerous individuals to share my findings. I am grateful to Jean Burgess at the Queensland University of Technology, Adam Lodders at the University of Melbourne, Michael Richardson at the University of New South Wales, and Alana Piper at the University of Technology Sydney. My ideas were still very much in development at the time, and the conversations at these venues did so much to help hone my arguments. In Australia, Chao Sun assisted with data wrangling for visualizations that helped me understand the editing of the 2011 Egyptian revolutions article on Wikipedia. And a grant by the University of New South Wales enabled me to work with Simon Taylor, who helped with data analysis and chatted endlessly with me about the exciting things we were learning.

Although other academics have been critical for my development as a researcher, I would have produced nothing if it were not for the many dedicated Wikipedians whom I have met and talked to about Wikipedia over the past decade. Special thanks to Dror Kamir, who in our many hours of conversation taught me so much about what it is like to be a Wikipedian in the Middle East; to the participants of the Oxford Internet Institute's "Wikipedia in the Middle East" project in Egypt and Jordan, including Farah Mustaklem and Mohamed Ouda; and to Jake Orlowitz, whose unfailing optimism continues to motivate me.

Thanks also to all the Wikipedians who talked with me about their experiences editing Wikipedia during the revolution—including Silver seren and Aude. Dario Taraborelli was a great source of support in my work involving citations in the knowledge graph, and I'm grateful, too, to the Wikimedia Foundation for listening to my criticisms and suggestions with an open ear. Thanks to Jimmy Wales for his support of Wikipedia in South Africa in my tenure as iCommons director and for his passion to diversify the movement.

My development editor, Craig Hillsley, was encouraging and supportive, even when I sent him an embarrassing first draft. He helped me see the bigger picture in the morass. My editor, Katie Helke, propelled the final edits to the manuscript that made it so much better. She was incredibly understanding and patient, and I'm grateful for her enthusiasm and encouragement. Thank you to my parents for their infinite love and support. This book simply would not have existed without you. Enorme grazie to my wonderful husband and partner, Luigi, whose help during writing with a new baby made this book possible, and to my beautiful boy, my precious, my kindred spirit, Salvatore. I dedicate this book to you both.

My final acknowledgments must be to the many young Egyptians who inspired this book. Especial thanks to The Egyptian Liberal for talking to me so openly after his initial reluctance. And a last word for Alaa Abdel Fattah, who was a colleague and friend during my time as a free and open source activist. Alaa is an icon of the revolution and a great Wikipedia supporter but remains imprisoned and tortured by the Egyptian authorities. His fight for democracy continues to inspire me.

NOTES

FOREWORD

1. Blake Montgomery, Ryan Mac, and Charlie Warzel, "YouTube Said It Will Link to Wikipedia Excerpts on Conspiracy Videos—but It Didn't Tell Wikipedia," *BuzzFeed News*, March 13, 2018, https://www.buzzfeednews.com/article/blakemontgomery/youtube-will-link-to-wikipedia-below-conspiracy-theory.

PREFACE

1. Wikipedia had previously been licensed under the GNU Free Documentation License, designed by the Free Software Foundation for the GNU project with similar rights as the Creative Commons Attribution Share-Alike license, which Wikipedia is currently licensed under.

2. Alana Semuels, "Is There a Boycott of Wikimania 2008?," *Los Angeles Times*, July 10, 2008, https://web.archive.org/web/20110519183750/http://latimesblogs.latimes.com/technology/2008/07/boycott-wikiman.html.

3. "Wikimania in Egypt," *Brian Lehrer Show*, July 25, 2008, https://www.wnyc.org/story/28223-wikimania-in-egypt.

4. Chris Taylor, "Why Not Call It a Facebook Revolution?," CNN.com, February 24, 2011, http://edition.cnn.com/2011/TECH/social.media/02/24/facebook.revolution/index.html.

5. Dror Kamir, "Egypte, brûle-t-elle?," January 31, 2011, http://listcultures.org/pipermail/cpov_listcultures.org/2011-January/000316.html.

6. CPOV (Critical Point of View) was a project led by the Institute for Network Cultures in the Netherlands and was dedicated to serious analysis and informed critique of Wikipedia.

7. Dror Kamir, "Egypte, brûle-t-elle?" from the CPOV mailing list, January 31, 2011, http://listcultures.org/pipermail/cpov_listcultures.org/2011-January/000316.html.

8. "What Wikipedia Is Not," English Wikipedia, https://en.wikipedia.org/w/index.php?title=Wikipedia:What_Wikipedia_is_not&oldid=1022619854.

9. Dror Kamir, "Parallel 'Online' and 'Real World' Egyptian Revolutions, or Wikipedia's Tahrir Square," Dror Kamir's blog, June 25, 2011, https://anduraru.wordpress.com/2011/06/25/parallel-online-and-real-world-egyptian-revolutions-or-wikipedias-tahrir-square/.

10. See, for example, Tarleton Gillespie, *Custodians of the Internet: Platforms, Content Moderation, and the Hidden Decisions That Shape Social Media* (Yale University Press, 2018).

CHAPTER 1

1. Amit Singhal, "Introducing the Knowledge Graph: Things, Not Strings," *The Keyword (blog)*, May 16, 2012, https://www.blog.google/products/search/introducing-knowledge-graph-things-not/.

2. Wikimedia Russia is a chapter of the Wikimedia Foundation for volunteers who contribute to Wikipedia and related projects in Russia. See https://meta.wikimedia.org/wiki/Wikimedia_Russia.

3. Singhal, "Introducing the Knowledge Graph."

4. See, for example, Luke Richards, "Why Wikipedia Is Still Visible across Google's SERPs in 2018," Search Engine Watch, November 13, 2018, https://www.searchenginewatch.com/2018/11/13/why-wikipedia-is-still-visible-across-googles-serps-in-2018/.

5. Michel Foucault, *Power/Knowledge: Selected Interviews and Other Writings, 1972–1977* (Harvester Wheatsheaf, 1980), 131.

6. Wikipedia consensus, https://en.wikipedia.org/w/index.php?title=Wikipedia:Consensus&oldid=1065640349.

7. Christopher Moldes, "Why Wait? Wikipedia and Google Accidentally Declare Putin the Winner of March 2018 Presidential Elections," Global Voices, January 16, 2018, https://globalvoices.org/2018/01/16/why-wait-wikipedia-and-google-accidentally-declare-putin-the-winner-of-march-2018-presidential-elections/.

8. James Surowiecki, *The Wisdom of Crowds* (Anchor, 2005).

9. Mary Morgan, "Traveling Facts," in *How Well Do Facts Travel? The Dissemination of Reliable Knowledge*, ed. Peter Howlett and Mary Morgan (Cambridge University Press, 2010), 3–42.

10. Robin Wagner-Pacifici, *What Is an Event?* (University of Chicago Press, 2017), 75.

11. Jimmy Wales, "Wikipedia Founder Jimmy Wales Responds," Slashdot, July 28, 2004, https://slashdot.org/story/04/07/28/1351230/wikipedia-founder-jimmy-wales-responds.

12. Pablo Beytía and Claudia Wagner, "Visibility Layers: A Framework for Facing the Complexity of the Gender Gap in Wikipedia Content," SocArXiv, December 18, 2020, https://doi.org/10.31235/osf.io/5ndkm.

13. Ruediger Glott and Rishab Ghosh, *Analysis of Wikipedia Survey Data*, United Nations University MERIT, 2010; Benjamin Mako Hill and Aaron Shaw, "The Wikipedia Gender Gap Revisited: Characterizing Survey Response Bias with Propensity Score Estimation," *PLoS ONE* 8, no. 6 (June 26, 2013): e65782, https://doi.org/10.1371/journal.pone.0065782; Shyong (Tony) K. Lam, Anuradha Uduwage, Zhenhua Dong, Shilad Sen, David R. Musicant, Loren Terveen, and John Riedl, "WP:Clubhouse? An Exploration of Wikipedia's Gender Imbalance," In *Proceedings of the 7th international symposium on wikis and open collaboration*, 2011, 1–10.

14. Mark Graham, Bernie Hogan, Ralph K. Straumann, and Ahmed Medhat, "Uneven Geographies of User-Generated Information: Patterns of Increasing Informational Poverty," *Annals of the Association of American Geographers* 104, no. 4 (2014): 746–764.

15. Beytía and Wagner, "Visibility Layers."

16. Heather Ford and Denny Vrandečić, "Automated Facts, Data Contextualization and Knowledge Colonialism: A Conversation between Denny Vrandečić and Heather Ford on Wikipedia's 20th Anniversary," *Big Data and Society Journal Blog*, December 10, 2020, http://bigdatasociety.net/.

17. Richard Cooke, "Wikipedia Is the Last Best Place on the Internet," *Wired*, February 17, 2020, https://www.wired.com/story/wikipedia-online-encyclopedia-best-place-internet/.

18. "Top 25 Report," Wikipedia, accessed March 22, 2021, https://en.wikipedia.org/wiki/Wikipedia:Top_25_Report/Number-one_articles#2021.

19. Brian Keegan, Darren Gergle, and Noshir Contractor, "Hot off the Wiki: Structures and Dynamics of Wikipedia's Coverage of Breaking News Events," *American Behavioral Scientist* 57, no. 5 (May 2013): 595–622, https://doi.org/10.1177/0002764212469367.

20. Paddy Scannell, "Media Events," *Media, Culture & Society* 17, no. 1 (1995): 154.

21. Cited in Paolo Gerbaudo, *Tweets and the Streets: Social Media and Contemporary Activism* (Pluto Press, 2012), 3.

22. Gerbaudo, *Tweets and the Streets*, 1–5.

23. Michela Ferron and Paolo Massa, "The Arab Spring | WikiRevolutions: Wikipedia as a Lens for Studying the Real-Time Formation of Collective Memories of Revolutions," *International Journal of Communication* 5 (2011): 20.

24. Christian Pentzold, "Fixing the Floating Gap: The Online Encyclopaedia Wikipedia as a Global Memory Place," *Memory Studies* 2, no. 2 (2009): 255–272.

25. Dariusz Jemielniak, *Common Knowledge? An Ethnography of Wikipedia* (Stanford University Press, 2014).

26. Marlon Twyman, Brian C. Keegan, and Aaron Shaw, "Black Lives Matter in Wikipedia: Collective Memory and Collaboration around Online Social Movements," in

Proceedings of the 2017 ACM Conference on Computer Supported Cooperative Work and Social Computing (2017): 1400–1412.

27. Ethnography is a research methodology that tries to understand the practices and cultures of the people being analyzed, typically through conducting interviews and observations. Although it originated in the field of anthropology, where ethnography was used to understand foreign populations, ethnography is often the method selected by science and technology studies for understanding knowledge systems and by digital media scholars for understanding the cultures and platforms of digital and social media platforms.

CHAPTER 2

1. Merlyna Lim, "Framing Bouazizi: 'White Lies', Hybrid Network, and Collective/Connective Action in the 2010–11 Tunisian Uprising," *Journalism* 14, no. 7 (2013): 921–941.

2. Lim, "Framing Bouazizi," 928.

3. Jon Leyne, "No Sign Egypt Will Take the Tunisian Road," BBC News, January 17, 2011, http://www.bbc.co.uk/news/world-middle-east-12202937.

4. Abigail Hauslohner, "After Tunisia: Why Egypt Isn't Ready to Have Its Own Revolution," *Time*, January 20, 2011, http://content.time.com/time/world/article/0,8599,2043497,00.html.

5. Wael Ghonim, "Wael Ghonim: Creating a 'Revolution 2.0' in Egypt," interview by Terry Gross, *Fresh Air*, NPR, February 9, 2012, https://www.npr.org/2012/02/09/146636605/wael-ghonim-creating-a-revolution-2-0-in-egypt.

6. Ghonim, "Creating a 'Revolution 2.0' in Egypt."

7. Xeni Jardin, "Egypt: The Viral Vlog of Asmaa Mahfouz That Helped Spark an Uprising," *BoingBoing*, February 2, 2011, https://boingboing.net/2011/02/02/egypt-the-viral-vlog.html.

8. Jardin, "Egypt."

9. Jardin, "Egypt."

10. Ruediger Glott and Rishab Ghosh, Analysis of Wikipedia Survey Data, United Nations University MERIT, 2010; Shyong (Tony) K. Lam, Anuradha Uduwage, Zhenhua Dong, Shilad W. Sen, David R. Musicant, Loren Terveen, and John Riedl, "WP:Clubhouse? An Exploration of Wikipedia's Gender Imbalance," in *Proceedings of the 7th International Symposium on Wikis and Open Collaboration* (Association for Computing Machinery, 2011), 1–10, https://doi.org/10.1145/2038558.2038560; Benjamin Mako Hill and Aaron Shaw, "The Wikipedia Gender Gap Revisited: Characterizing Survey Response Bias with Propensity Score Estimation," *PLoS ONE* 8, no. 6 (June 26, 2013): e65782.

11. Wikimedia Foundation, *Wikipedia Editors Study: Results from the Editor Survey, April 2011*, 2011, https://upload.wikimedia.org/wikipedia/commons/7/76/Editor_Survey_Report_-_April_2011.pdf.

12. Ruediger Glott, Philipp Schmidt, and Rishab Ghosh, *Wikipedia Survey: Overview of Results*, UNU-MERIT, 2010, https://web.archive.org/web/20110728182835/http://www.wikipediastudy.org/docs/Wikipedia_Overview_15March2010-FINAL.pdf.

13. "Monthly Overview," Wikimedia Statistics, accessed January 20, 2021, https://stats.wikimedia.org/.

14. Wikimedia Foundation, "Wikipedia Founder Jimmy Wales Leads South African Wikipedia Academies in Johannesburg," press release, October 31, 2007, https://foundation.wikimedia.org/wiki/Press_releases/Wikipedia_Academies.

15. Wikimedia Foundation, *Wikipedia Editors Survey*.

16. Shilad W. Sen, Heather Ford, David R. Musicant, Mark Graham, Os Keyes, and Brent Hecht, "Barriers to the Localness of Volunteered Geographic information," in *Proceedings of the 33rd Annual ACM Conference on Human Factors in Computing Systems* (Association for Computing Machinery, 2015), 197–206, https://doi.org/10.1145/2702123.2702170.

17. Heather Ford, Elizabeth Dubois, and Cornelius Puschmann, "Keeping Ottawa Honest—One Tweet at a Time? Politicians, Journalists, Wikipedians and Their Twitter Bots," in "Automation, Algorithms, and Politics," special issue, *International Journal of Communication* 10 (2016): 24.

18. "Please do not bite the newcomers," English Wikipedia, https://en.wikipedia.org/w/index.php?title=Wikipedia:Please_do_not_bite_the_newcomers&oldid=1032557097.

19. Aaron Halfaker, R. Stuart Geiger, Jonathan T. Morgan, and John Riedl, "The Rise and Decline of an Open Collaboration System: How Wikipedia's Reaction to Popularity Is Causing Its Decline," *American Behavioral Scientist* 57, no. 5 (2013): 664–688.

20. The Egyptian Liberal, interview by the author, October 14, 2012.

21. The Egyptian Liberal, interview, October 14, 2012.

22. "What Wikipedia Is Not," English Wikipedia, https://en.wikipedia.org/w/index.php?title=Wikipedia:What_Wikipedia_is_not&oldid=1020477037.

23. Brian C. Keegan, "A History of Newswork on Wikipedia," in *Proceedings of the 9th International Symposium on Open Collaboration* (Association for Computing Machinery, 2013), 7.

24. See the archive at http://web.archive.org/web/20060111221201/http://sep11.wikipedia.org/wiki/Main_Page.

25. See the edits at "Wikipedia:What Wikipedia is not," English Wikipedia, https://en.wikipedia.org/w/index.php?title=Wikipedia:What_Wikipedia_is_not&diff=next&oldid=147823.

26. Available at "Wikipedia:What Wikipedia is not," English Wikipedia, https://en.wikipedia.org/w/index.php?title=Wikipedia:What_Wikipedia_is_not&diff=prev&oldid=149521.

27. "Wikipedia:What Wikipedia Is Not."

28. "Wikipedia:Notability," English Wikipedia, https://en.wikipedia.org/wiki/Wikipedia:Notability.

29. "Wikipedia:Notability (Events)," English Wikipedia, https://en.wikipedia.org/w/index.php?title=Wikipedia:Notability_(events)&oldid=1038377199.

30. "Articles for deletion: Kenyan invasion of Somalia," English Wikipedia, https://en.wikipedia.org/w/index.php?title=Wikipedia:Articles_for_deletion/Kenyan_invasion_of_Somalia_(2011)&oldid=456971363.

31. "Articles for deletion: Kenyan invasion of Somalia."

32. "Articles for deletion: Kenyan invasion of Somalia."

33. Donna Haraway, "Situated Knowledges: The Science Question in Feminism and the Privilege of Partial Perspective," *Feminist Studies* 14, no. 3 (1988): 575–599.

34. Nathaniel Tkacz, *Wikipedia and the Politics of Openness* (University of Chicago Press, 2015).

35. Tkacz, *Wikipedia and the Politics of Openness*, 78.

36. Nathaniel Tkacz, "La veritat de la Viquipèdia," *Digithum: Humanities in Digital Era* 14 (2012): 93.

CHAPTER 3

1. The first version of the article can be found at "2011 Egyptian revolution," English Wikipedia, https://en.wikipedia.org/w/index.php?title=Egyptian_revolution_of_2011&oldid=409962868.

2. The Article Wizard no longer contains these warnings about breaking news.

3. R. Stuart Geiger, "The Lives of Bots," in *Wikipedia: A Critical Point of View*, ed. Geert Lovink and Nathaniel Tkacz (Institute of Network Cultures, 2011), 78–93.

4. Robin Wagner-Pacifici, *What Is an Event?* (University of Chicago Press, 2017), 26.

5. "Wikipedia:Article Titles," English Wikipedia, https://en.wikipedia.org/w/index.php?title=Wikipedia:Article_titles&oldid=963665938.

6. See "Wikipedia:Naming Conventions (Events)," English Wikipedia, https://en.wikipedia.org/w/index.php?title=Wikipedia:Naming_conventions_(events)&oldid=945673136.

7. This wasn't always the case. Infoboxes on Wikipedia evolved from taxonomy infoboxes (or so-called taxoboxes) that editors developed to represent the scientific classification of organisms. The move by a group of editors to populate all articles with infoboxes was accompanied by heavy debate about whether all subjects could (or should) be easily reduced using these factual summaries.

8. "Infobox," English Wikipedia, https://en.wikipedia.org/w/index.php?title=Infobox&oldid=1035482361.

9. "Infobox," English Wikipedia.

10. One needs to view the source of the page in order to see all the fields of the infobox that were filled in since the template is no longer used and its display is now broken.

11. "The Media Line: About Us," accessed 23 January 2022, https://themedialine.org/about-our-vision/.

12. Wagner-Pacifici, *What Is an Event?*, 26.

13. The software for the New Pages Feed interface was enhanced by the Wikimedia Foundation in 2011, shortly after The Egyptian Liberal's article was first created, but its basic elements were still in place at the time.

14. The Egyptian Liberal, Lihaas user page, 13:31 UTC, January 25, 2011.

15. Heroeswithmetaphors, 2011 Egyptian protests talk page, 20:05 UTC, January 25, 2011.

16. See "Wikipedia: Wikiproject Orphanage," English Wikipedia, https://en.wikipedia.org/w/index.php?title=Wikipedia:WikiProject_Orphanage&oldid=1061690246.

17. The Egyptian Liberal, interview by the author, October 14, 2012.

18. Jonathan Dee, "All the News That's Fit to Print Out," *New York Times Sunday Magazine*, July 1, 2007.

19. Fernanda B. Viégas, Martin Wattenberg, and Dave Kushal, "Studying Cooperation and Conflict between Authors with *History Flow* Visualizations," in *Proceedings of the SIGCHI Conference on Human Factors in Computing Systems*, CHI '04 (Association for Computing Machinery, 2004): 580, https://doi.org/10.1145/985692.985765.

CHAPTER 4

1. The first version of the Arabic Wikipedia article can be found at https://ar.wikipedia.org/w/index.php?title=%20percentD8%20percentAB%20percentD9%20percent88%20percentD8%20percentB1%20percentD8%20percentA9_25_%20percentD9%20percent8A%20percentD9%20percent86%20percentD8%20percentA7%20percentD9%20percent8A%20percentD8%20percentB1&oldid=6321581 or https://bit.ly/2ZtOfHf.

2. Jake Orlowitz (Ocaasi), interview by the author, April 3, 2014.

3. Ocaasi has written about his Wikipedia experience in "How Wikipedia Drove Professors Crazy, Made Me Sane, and Almost Saved the Internet," in *Wikipedia@20*, ed. Joseph Reagle and Jackie Koerner (MIT Press, 2020), 125–140.

4. Ocaasi, interview, May 24, 2017.

5. Ocaasi, interview, May 24, 2017.

6. See "2011 Egyptian revolution: Difference between revisions," English Wikipedia, https://en.wikipedia.org/w/index.php?title=Egyptian_revolution_of_2011&diff=prev&oldid=410552437&diffmode=visual.

7. ClueBot NG is different from other antivandal bots. It isn't pre-programmed to recognize vandalism but rather learns what is considered vandalism by comparing the proposed edit against a data set of both vandalism and constructive edits. See "English Wikipedia:User:ClueBot_NG," https://en.wikipedia.org/wiki/User:ClueBot_NG/FAQ.

8. Heather Ford, Shilad W. Sen, David R. Musicant, and Nathaniel Miller, "Getting to the Source: Where Does Wikipedia Get Its Information From?," in *Proceedings of*

the 9th International Symposium on Open Collaboration, WikiSym '13 (Association for Computing Machinery, 2013), 9:1–9:10.

9. Shilad W. Sen, Heather Ford, David R. Musicant, Mark Graham, Oliver Keyes, and Brent Hecht, "Barriers to the Localness of Volunteered Geographic Information," in *Proceedings of the 33rd Annual ACM Conference on Human Factors in Computing Systems* (Association for Computing Machinery, 2015), 197–206.

10. Saba Bebawi, *Media Power and Global Television News: The Role of Al Jazeera English* (Bloomsbury Publishing, 2016).

11. Brian Stelter, "Al Jazeera English Finds an Audience," *New York Times*, January 31, 2011, http://www.nytimes.com/2011/02/01/world/middleeast/01jazeera.html.

12. David Folkenflik, "Clinton Lauds Al Jazeera: 'It's Real News,'" National Public Radio, March 3, 2011, http://www.npr.org/sections/thetwo-way/2011/03/03/134243115/clinton-lauds-virtues-of-al-jazeera-its-real-news.

13. Stelter, "Al Jazeera English Finds an Audience."

14. Mark Jurkowitz, "Events in Egypt Trigger Record Coverage," *Pew Research Center's Journalism Project* (blog), February 5, 2011, https://www.journalism.org/2011/02/05/pej-news-coverage-index-january-31-february-6-2011/.

15. Ocaasi, interview, April 3, 2014.

16. Ocaasi, interview, April 3, 2014.

17. 2011 Egyptian revolution talk page, February 6, 2011, English Wikipedia, https://en.wikipedia.org/w/index.php?title=Egyptian_revolution_of_2011&oldid=413356129.

18. 2011 Egyptian revolution talk page, February 2, 2011, English Wikipedia.

19. 2011 Egyptian revolution talk page, February 6, 2011, English Wikipedia.

20. 2011 Egyptian revolution talk page, February 6, 2011, English Wikipedia.

21. Ocaasi, interview, April 3, 2014.

22. 2011 Egyptian revolution talk page, January 29, 2011, English Wikipedia.

23. Aude, interview by the author, May 4, 2012.

24. Sometimes, the identity of editors themselves is obscure. In my interview with him, The Egyptian Liberal stated that he shared his Wikipedia user account with three other people in different countries during events in Egypt for security reasons (i.e., to try to trick the Egyptian authorities if they were able to discover his identity). "During the revolution it was not only me editing from the page. I had different people who didn't have an account on Wikipedia who wanted to edit Wikipedia especially at the time of the revolution they really wanted to help. So we were three different people with different writing styles. . . . The two that were helping most were not Egyptian." Interview, October 14, 2012.

CHAPTER 5

1. "Mubarak Refuses to Resign—Thursday 10 February," *The Guardian* (blog), February 10, 2011, https://www.theguardian.com/world/blog/2011/feb/10/egypt-hosni-mubarak-resignation-rumours.

2. Haroon Siddique, Paul Owen, and Richard Adams, "Mubarak Resigns—Friday 11 February," *The Guardian* (blog), February 11, 2011, http://www.theguardian.com/world/blog/2011/feb/11/egypt-hosni-mubarak-left-cairo.

3. Avi Issacharoff and News Agencies, "Mubarak Resigns as Egypt's President, Hands Power to Army," Haaretz, accessed February 11, 2011, https://www.haaretz.com/1.5121293.

4. Haroon Siddique, Paul Owen, and Richard Adams, "Mubarak Resigns—Friday 11 February," *The Guardian* (blog), February 11, 2011, http://www.theguardian.com/world/blog/2011/feb/11/egypt-hosni-mubarak-left-cairo.

5. "Wikipedia:Requested Moves," English Wikipedia, https://en.wikipedia.org/w/index.php?title=Wikipedia:Requested_moves&oldid=1035920009.

6. "Wikipedia:Requested Moves."

7. Christian Pentzold, "Fixing the Floating Gap: The Online Encyclopaedia Wikipedia as a Global Memory Place," *Memory Studies* 2, no. 2 (May 2009): 255–272, https://doi.org/10.1177/1750698008102055.

8. 2011 Egyptian revolution talk page, February 6, 2011, English Wikipedia, https://en.wikipedia.org/w/index.php?title=Egyptian_revolution_of_2011&oldid=413356129.

9. The article's title is changed to "revolution" earlier on the Arabic version of the encyclopedia. At 17:06 on February 11, just over an hour after the resignation is announced, an experienced Wikipedian, Mohamed_Ouda, makes the edit. It is changed much later in the Egyptian Arabic version (i.e., at 07:12 UTC on February 12), by Ghaly.

10. The edit is available at "2011 Egyptian revolution."

11. Émile Durkheim, *The Elementary Forms of the Religious Life* (George Allen & Unwin, 1915), https://www.gutenberg.org/files/41360/41360-h/41360-h.htm.

12. Heather Ford and Stuart Geiger Ford, "Writing up Rather Than Writing Down: Becoming Wikipedia Literate," in *Proceedings of the 8th Annual International Symposium on Wikis and Open Collaboration* (Association for Computing Machinery, 2012), 1–4.

13. Kate Crawford and Tarleton Gillespie, "What Is a Flag For? Social Media Reporting Tools and the Vocabulary of Complaint," *New Media & Society* 18, no. 3 (2016): 421.

14. Zeynep Tufekci, *Twitter and Tear Gas: The Power and Fragility of Networked Protest* (Yale University Press, 2017).

15. Robin Wagner-Pacifici, *What Is an Event?* (University of Chicago Press, 2017), 75.

16. Wagner-Pacifici, *What Is an Event?*, 155.

17. Tim Olaveson, "Collective Effervescence and Communitas: Processual Models of Ritual and Society in Emile Durkheim and Victor Turner," *Dialectical Anthropology* 26, no. 2 (2001): 89–124.

18. See John Langshaw Austin, *How to Do Things with Words*, William James Lectures (Oxford University Press, 1975).

CHAPTER 6

1. 2011 Egyptian revolution talk page, July 13, 2012, English Wikipedia, https://en.wikipedia.org/w/index.php?title=Egyptian_revolution_of_2011&oldid=413356129.

2. 2011 Egyptian revolution talk page, November 6, 2012.

3. Andreas Kolbe, "Whither Wikidata?," *The Signpost*, December 2, 2015, https://en.wikipedia.org/wiki/Wikipedia:Wikipedia_Signpost/2015-12-02/Op-ed.

4. Heather Ford, "Max Klein on Wikidata, 'Botpedia' and Gender Classification," *Hblog.Org* (blog), September 8, 2014, https://hblog.org/2014/09/08/max-klein-on-wikidata-botpedia-and-gender-classification/.

5. 2011 Egyptian revolution talk page, March 12, 2013, English Wikipedia.

6. There is little agreement in the literature about what distinguishes semantic networks, knowledge graphs, and knowledge bases. The latter two terms have been applied to both Wikidata and Google's knowledge graph. I use the term "semantic network" to encompass both the knowledge base and the knowledge graph.

7. Amit Singhal, "Introducing the Knowledge Graph: Things, Not Strings," *The Keyword* (blog), May 16, 2012, https://www.blog.google/products/search/introducing-knowledge-graph-things-not/.

8. Singhal, "Introducing the Knowledge Graph."

9. Connor McMahon, Isaac Johnson, and Brent Hecht, "The Substantial Interdependence of Wikipedia and Google: A Case Study on the Relationship between Peer Production Communities and Information Technologies," in *Proceedings of the 11th International Conference on Web and Social Media, ICWSM 2017* (AAAI Press, 2017), 142–151.

10. Dario Taraborelli, email correspondence with the author, August 31, 2019.

11. Rachel Abrams, "Google Thinks I'm Dead," *New York Times*, December 16, 2017, https://www.nytimes.com/2017/12/16/business/google-thinks-im-dead.html.

12. "Wikipedia:Village pump policy archive:Discussion re Verifiability issues with Wikidata," English Wikipedia, https://en.wikipedia.org/w/index.php?title=Wikipedia:Village_pump_(policy)/Archive_128&oldid=1064387603.

13. "Wikipedia:Village," English Wikipedia.

14. Mark Graham, "The Problem with Wikidata," *The Atlantic*, April 6, 2012, https://www.theatlantic.com/technology/archive/2012/04/the-problem-with-wikidata/255564/.

15. Ford, "Max Klein on Wikidata."

16. See my chapter "Rise of the Underdog," in *Wikipedia@20*, ed. Joseph Reagle and Jackie Koerner (MIT Press, 2021), 189–201.

17. Dario Taraborelli, interview by the author, July 19, 2019.

18. Quoted in Caitlin Dewey, "You Probably Haven't Even Noticed Google's Sketchy Quest to Control the World's Knowledge," *Washington Post*, May 11, 2016, https://www.washingtonpost.com/news/the-intersect/wp/2016/05/11/you-probably-havent-even-noticed-googles-sketchy-quest-to-control-the-worlds-knowledge/.

19. "What Is Provenance?," World Wide Web Consortium, accessed June 29, 2020, https://www.w3.org/2005/Incubator/prov/wiki/index.php?title=What_Is_Provenance&oldid=2026.

20. Tim Berners-Lee, James Hendler, and Ora Lassila, "The Semantic Web," *Scientific American*, May 17, 2001, http://www.scientificamerican.com/article.cfm?id=the-semantic-web.

21. Mike Bergman, "A Common Sense View of Knowledge Graphs," *mkbergman.com* (blog), July 1, 2019, https://www.mkbergman.com/2244/a-common-sense-view-of-knowledge-graphs/.

22. Mike Ananny and Kate Crawford, "Seeing without Knowing: Limitations of the Transparency Ideal and Its Application to Algorithmic Accountability," *New Media & Society* 20, no. 3 (March 1, 2018): 974, https://doi.org/10.1177/1461444816676645.

23. See, for example, Neil Thurman, Judith Moeller, Natali Helberger, and Damian Trilling, "My Friends, Editors, Algorithms, and I," *Digital Journalism* 7, no. 4 (2018): 447–469, https://doi.org/10.1080/21670811.2018.1493936.

CHAPTER 7

1. The Egyptian Liberal, interview by the author, February 2017.

2. Ocaasi, interview by the author, May 2017.

3. Daniel Dayan and Elihu Katz, *Media Events* (Harvard University Press, 1992).

4. Dayan and Katz, *Media Events*, 217.

5. See Andreas Hepp and Nick Couldry, "Introduction: Media Events in Globalized Media Cultures," in *Media Events in a Global Age*, ed. Andreas Hepp and Nick Couldry (Routledge, 2009), 1–20.

6. Dariusz Jemielniak, *Common Knowledge? An Ethnography of Wikipedia* (Stanford University Press, 2014).

7. Marlon Twyman, Brian C. Keegan, and Aaron Shaw, "Black Lives Matter in Wikipedia: Collective Memory and Collaboration around Online Social Movements," in *Proceedings of the 2017 ACM Conference on Computer Supported Cooperative Work and Social Computing* (Association for Computing Machinery, 2017), 1400–1412.

8. Caitlyn Dewey, "You Probably Haven't Even Noticed Google's Sketchy Quest to Control the World's Knowledge," *Washington Post*, April 26, 2019.

9. Donna Haraway, "Situated Knowledges: The Science Question in Feminism and the Privilege of Partial Perspective," *Feminist Studies* 14, no. 3 (1988): 581.

INDEX